THE END OF MY SOAP OPERA LIFE

DEATH OF THE SUN

SAM

Sixth Edition

Copyright © 2014

All rights reserved.

ISBN 978-1-939890-29-0

Brief quotations embodied in critical articles and reviews allowed. Include the book's title, author's name, and the Lightworker's Log web site (LightworkersLog.com) as sources of further information. Contact the author via the above web site to comment, for written permission regarding longer excerpts, or to otherwise use or reproduce this book.

Comments in this book are based on the author's perception only. The author makes no warranties as to the accuracy, completeness, timeliness or usefulness of any information in this book. The author and all parties associated with the book are not responsible for any of the information in it. In using this book, you agree that any party involved in creating, producing or delivering it, is not liable for any of the information within. You are solely responsible if you use any of the information in this book for any purpose.

Because of the dynamic nature of the Internet, web addresses or links contained in this book may have changed since publication and may no longer be valid.

Dedicated to family and friends, especially those mentioned here. Your lessons were very valuable in helping me to grow. I will be forever grateful to you for sharing your life with me. I learned there is so much more to life than anyone could ever know.

Let the power games end and look within.

Acknowledgments

This book would not exist without the help of many people. Everyone noted within these pages taught me valuable lessons. I will always be grateful for them. Family, friends, and spiritual teachers met through classes, workshops, seminars, and conferences all helped to make this book possible. I remain grateful for that entity many people call God.

A special thank you to the beloved ones who helped to edit the book before publication: Karen Bellesky, Nancy Brooks, Deane Edelman, Marty Howard, Rev. Jean Yzer and Ray Pilara.

Contents

Preface	vii
Author's Insight	xi

Chapters

1-The Ultimate Drama	1
2-Preparing for Change	9
3-Sherman's Ultimate Gift	15
4- Daddy Wins the Lotto	21
5-The Nightmare Continues	37
6-Shock City	43
7-Big Changes Ahead	53
8-Time to Wake Up	69
9-The Last Visit	77
10-The Aftermath	83
11-Woo, Woo Times	95
12-Family at Play	103
13-More Time to Grieve	109
14-New Life Begins	119

15-Spirit Contacts	129
16-Confirmation at Last	137
17-Revelations	147
18-The Burden Increases	159
19-Drama All Around	165
20-Christmas Holiday Begins	173
21-Christmas Holiday Ends	189
Epilogue	197
Bibliography	199
About the Author	201

Preface

Most people thought I went crazy when my son, Daniel, died. Some still believe I live in the twilight zone. I've had what many people would consider a full and colorful life and kept track of almost everything that occurred. Journals, poems, family pictures, videos, and recorded voices of family members helped me to write this book.

At 40-years-old, I started thinking about writing my life story. Things are finally becoming more in focus now that I'm 57-years-old. There's an urgent need to share my struggles, joys, and resulting growth in book form. Sharing the odd things that happened will help others and myself.

I've been trying to decide what kind of book to write for years. The book I started to write, a long time ago, would take me back, causing me to relive many of the worst years of this life. Now I know better. This book is about what Samantha experienced. I thought I was she but since my way of thinking changed, I'm not the same person as before. Since I'm not Samantha, this book is written in the third person.

Samantha never paid much attention to what other people thought or how she conducted her life. So how did a Detroit-born girl from the projects get to Florida? The answer is both simple and complicated.

Samantha grew by following her intuition and going through a lot of struggle, a lot of pain, and a lot of joy. She never stopped to consider how to fill her day but always read plenty of books, mainly romance novels to stop thinking about her own life. Samantha never considered what she was doing or why she did it. The idea of cause and effect never entered her mind. She never thought about the consequences of her actions. "Work hard, party hard," was her motto.

Ralph Waldo Emerson once said, "Do not go where the path may lead, go instead where there is no path and leave a trail." Always defiant, Samantha chose to blaze her own trail, disregarding paths taken by the masses. Samantha believed humans lived many lives and there was a lesson in everything. But she never thought about how her choices affected others or if other people might follow her path. Daniel followed her lead.

Throughout life, she very rarely second-guessed her own judgment but mostly believed in her own ability to do anything to which she set her mind to do. Samantha learned at an early age that all things are just a matter of time and effort. She learned quickly to work for what she wanted when caught after stealing a red, mohair sweater at 10-years-old. Other lessons took much longer to learn.

Many unusual things happened to Samantha. But she accomplished a whole lot more than she ever dared to dream, as every major goal became reality. Samantha rose above years of having little food to eat to being middle class and eating whatever desired. She never regretted relationships, even when abusive, but grew from the appearance of victim to forgiveness and love for all people. She learned that lust and passion often lead people astray because sometimes what we think of as love betrays our inner core. Now she knows these are chances to learn valuable lessons. We also have chances to bring children into this world. Newborns are pure, God-conscious points of white light sent to lead us. Samantha learned that humans are not meant to live in limitation. This lesson was hard to learn as she married and divorced three times. She nearly died several times through attempted suicide and major illnesses. Now she realizes that in essence she is perfect, whole, and complete.

Birthing a son at sixteen and a daughter seven years later were godsends to Samantha's growth. The perception of losing her son was the greatest thing that ever happened to her as his physical death woke her up. His spirit then helped her to turn so-called tragedy and loss into the best years of her life. She quickly learned to follow intuition and gut feelings and now listens to the voices inside her head that she believes are members of her spirit group. The voices are directed by a Supreme Being, whatever you care to call *It;* it is all God. Once we come to *It*, God guides our every thought and action towards the greater good of all.

Humanity lives in a dream world and it's time to **wake-up**. There are many new age books on spirituality and people publish more every day. Samantha began to read them after her son's transition. Some books made sense but she didn't agree with everything read. She realized that most authors write for people who think as they do.

This book helps Samantha to stay in tune with a new way of thinking. She is an evolving spirit, a teacher of God. *The End of My Soap Opera Life* reaches people at different levels of awareness. It lets them know <u>there is much more to life than anyone can ever know</u>. The book helps people to open their minds to greater ideas and is about waking up from the dream. If you decide it's not for you, please give this book to someone else. It will reach the people it's meant to reach.

The book begins more than a year before Samantha was reborn and starts with the so-called death of her son Daniel. It mentions times of connection to loved ones in other planes. And it notes times when life just continued to seem unbearable until Samantha finally recognized the Truth and began to change her perception of life as we know it.

Although there are numerous references to things that happened to Samantha, the book is not about her. However, it is written as is because we all seem to relate more to personal experience. Maybe that's why Samantha documented so much of her life, to write this book and help more people to **wake-up**. Unseen Beings wait on the other side of the veil of illusion. We need only to ask them to help us, and they will. But we must be careful to ask only for the *Lights of God*.

Readers can skip *Author's Notes* (in italics at the end of chapters) until ready to read them. They deal with the author's beliefs at the time she wrote the book. They are also about lessons learned or revelations the author had after certain life situations. No matter what state of awareness the reader may be in, there truly is something for everyone who reads this book. You are blessed, and oh, so very loved!

Each day is a gift to relish by doing what is right even though everyone's perspective of what is "right" seems different. Samantha continues to recognize the unseen forces guiding her each day. She knows there's only one force, and in America, it is called God. She asks for daily guidance knowing that more and more people are beginning to seek God now too.

Thoughts are indeed things as Ernest Holmes teaches in *The Science of Mind*. Humans are born to live lives of joy and abundance. Samantha learned that after fifty-seven years on earth and is now passing that message on to you. As Ernest Holmes wrote in 1926:

"The day will come when people will choose the thoughts that they allow to enter the mind as carefully as they now choose the food they eat. Staying close to the thought of the One Mind is a safe and sure protection from any and all wrong mental influence."

:-)

Author's Insight

"My pre-birth vision into this life was designed to teach. To teach, I must learn. To learn, I had to suffer. I am now done with suffering. It is time to teach here, in this life, on this plane."

Readers must consider the contents of this book from their own level of awareness. The levels of awareness, of understanding, are different for everyone. Some readers may be interested in learning more about certain subjects by getting the references listed in the back of the book. While many people believe that we can communicate with our departed loved ones, knowing that it's all God helps to more easily understand the lessons learned by Samantha. We are all parts of God and need only recognize this truth to improve our lives.

Numbers in the text of the book identify *Author's Notes* at the end of each chapter. It is vital to read them for they deal with lessons learned or revelations the author had after certain life situations. The book can be depressing without the insights in the *Author's Notes*. Reading these notes helps the reader to understand that a path to peace and light was slowly emerging to guide Samantha.

There is much more to life than anyone knows. This is clear by the end of the book.

:-)

~ 1 ~
The Ultimate Drama

The telephone rings loudly as Samantha tosses in bed hoping it will stop. After sleeping in the living room chair for hours, it feels as if she just crawled into bed. The nightstand alarm clock shows it's barely five o'clock in the morning. It has to be someone with an urgent message, or need, and she hopes it has nothing to do with either her son or daughter. A sense of doom fills the air as she moves quickly toward the telephone in her home office. Samantha's husband, James, stirs but does not rise as she picks up the receiver.

"Daniel is dead," Joy, her son's mother-in-law, yells through the receiver with a panic-filled voice.

Joy's frequent harmful actions towards Samantha always leave her filled with rage. Today is no different as she reacts immediately filled with anger.

"You're f**king with me again, aren't you," Samantha snarls sarcastically.

"No he's really dead. The state police just left. Rachel asked me to call because she's too upset to talk to anyone."

Rachel, Daniel's wife, is in shock. James rises to hear Samantha's side of the conversation. Samantha refuses to believe Joy and asks for more information to verify her story. Joy tells her the name of the state police officer at the scene of the accident. To this day, she still can't recall if she ever thanked Joy for being the one to tell her of Daniel's death. [1]

After many calls, Samantha finally speaks to the female sheriff who arrived on the scene shortly after the accident. She asks to see her son. The sheriff promptly tells her all she can do now is contact a funeral parlor. Daniel's distinctive wizard tattoo, and his wallet identification, positively identifies him.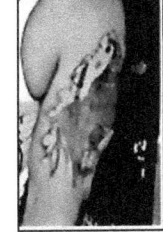

No one, not even his mother, can see his body.

The officer's report is very specific. Daniel rode his motorcycle at more than 100 miles per hour before hitting the rear of a vehicle in front of him. He was tossed from the bike upon impact. Witnesses reported that he died "almost instantly." Sheriffs already delivered personal belongings to his wife Rachel at their South Florida home.

Samantha's heart pounds loudly. Rage fills her body. Her chest heaves as she begins to hyperventilate and gasp for air. The drama is on and it increases with each thought of the past. (2) She hangs up the telephone feeling overwhelmed with a complete and total sense of loss. Uncontrollable crying begins as she falls to the floor.

The agony comes from deep inside her gut. Sobs seem to heave, up and out, making her stomach and throat tremble. James stands in the room with her. He seems confused and looks around trying to decide what to do. Finally, he sits down on the black futon as she cries uncontrollably hunched up on the floor two feet away.

They stay there for thirty minutes, until Samantha can cry no more. She can't bear to tell her daughter Rebecca who is ill with a mysterious illness. Rebecca hasn't slept well for a long time. This Palm Sunday marks the last time she will try to sleep in the innocence of not knowing Daniel, her protector, is dead. It is so unlike the joyous Sunday mornings when they both were born.

Samantha wants Rebecca to have a few more hours of precious sleep. Her sister, Ruth, is usually up for work very early so she calls her. Ruth answers the phone within seconds and listens in stunned silence as Samantha bawls about Daniel's untimely death. Ruth is the one that tells Rebecca her beloved brother is dead. Naomi, Ruth's partner, stays with Rebecca's 12-year-old son, Samuel, while the two women race to James and Samantha's house in Ruth's black, Chevy van. Through sobs, Samantha tells them what she knows of Daniel's accident. They cry together on the screened-in back porch as the sun rises in the South Florida sky.

Samantha already misses Daniel's infectious smile and looking into his sensitive, hazel eyes that look like hers. Daniel was always attentive to everyone but still traveled to the beat of his own drum. Truly a free spirit, he displayed the freedom she and others could not seem to grasp. Except for the last few years of life, he always seemed to be the one having the most fun, enjoying each moment lived to the fullest. Even as pain immobilizes Samantha, she's thankful to have given birth to him and thankful for his love, which she continues to sense.

Many mystics note love is the force that brings the greatest effect. Love is the state of BEing, Dr. Page tells us, a willingness to merge and connect without mental force. A state of wholeness reflects in the individual within this force of love. We are then able to commune outside of time and space. In time, the love Daniel and Samantha hold helps Samantha to break through the veil of forgetfulness. But for now, Samantha is especially thankful that he set up the situation of his death making it so much easier for everyone that knew him. No one has to go through the trauma of identifying his 5' 6" body. [3]

Daniel played his human life role well as a sensitive and caring individual. People always noted his generosity, cheerful presence, unending kindness, and love. He was a great son, a great peacemaker, a great friend and father to Samantha who will be grateful to his essence, in future years, for helping her to realize we are all a part of God.

Samantha will soon learn there is nothing separate from the Creator of all living things. It is only in our beliefs, in this dream that we call human life, where we think we are actually in a mind-body. In later years, Samantha will only allow herself to miss him for short times. Then she will remember what Daniel tells her several months after passing from human form.

"Forget about me Mom, I never was and never will be."

Yet, loved ones are never lost. Consciousness transcends all space weaving both to and from the physical plane. Love is an unbreakable connection, Emmanuel notes, that passes through every illusory barrier, even time and space. Once we believe that we exist beyond the physical world we will be in contact with the ones we love. And it will be more real than the physicality touched before. Samantha will soon begin to enjoy many experiences when Daniel's spirit returns to be with her. Daniel's spirit will guide her for years to come.

But for now, Daniel's family weeps as the heat of Sunday morning raises, so unlike the cold February day when he was born. Pinwheels of blame began to turn. [4]

Samantha solemnly distributes copies of four sheets of paper given to Daniel on the last day she saw him alive. She feels they have something to do with his death. Rebecca and Ruth read in silence. They then sit talking as tears continue to fall. It seems impossible to stop blaming everyone for Daniel's death. [5]

The details of separation, family violence and fear reappear as Samantha searches for answers. Daniel's death spurs a strong desire to seek the real meaning of life as she begins her quest for self-mastery. Thankfully, she will soon read *Celestine Prophecy* by James Redfield, which notes a Fifth Insight to life that helps us raise our vibration level (celestinevision.com). This insight heralds an inner connection with Divine Energy and marks the end of insecurity and violence. Unknowingly, Samantha now moves quickly towards knowledge of the Fifth Insight.

1. Samantha thinks certain people are in her life for a reason. Although she can't determine why Joy now plays such a prominent role, she knows their predestined relationship has a purpose. It comforts her to know that other people hold similar beliefs upon reading John Edwards's book *One Last Time*.

    We live many different lives, each planned before birth, based on what our soul desires to experience. The primary goal of life is to experience and express unconditional love. Humans take turns living "good guy" and "bad guy" roles and in this life Joy appears to play a great "bad guy" role, a role Samantha played in many previous lives. Samantha will soon learn that Joy is in essence her spiritual friend and ally. Joy's soul agreed to play her role to help them meet the primary goal of life because of their eternal love for one another.

    Joy is Samantha's "special hate" relationship but she will not know this until she becomes a student of *A Course in Miracles*. Now immersed in their perceived hate for one another, Samantha doesn't recognize she and Joy are unique parts of God, helping one another to learn the primary lesson of unconditional love. She will learn in time that everyone is innocent because we are in a dream world. Samantha will bless Joy for playing such a pivotal role in their lives and for helping Daniel to realize his true nature.

    Daniel is Samantha's "special love" relationship, for she loves him more than she loves anyone else, even God. Samantha believes Daniel completes her and will always be there for her. In her denial of Truth, he is the only love that will always love her.

    A Course in Miracles notes: "When you make something to fill a perceived lack, you are tacitly implying that you believe in separation." Not recognizing her oneness with God as a human, Samantha gave birth to a son who would remind her, when he died, that we are all parts of God. Close in age, they grew up together, feeling an uncomfortable sense of loss when physically apart. Yet, her task to alert others to the Truth would begin upon his death.

    Later, with clarity of mind, Samantha knows their souls planned this event before birth on earth. It takes her years to understand why but she eventually recognizes how minute details of Daniel's passing made the experience of waking-up from the dream of earth life easier. Bearing the tragic human loss of a son, Samantha also realizes that, as a soul, Daniel's death is the best thing that ever happened to her.

We promise to learn, Dr. Christine Page reminds us, believing the illusion of this world, until we accomplish sacred contracts. We agree to abide by earth rules after making bargains "with others to turn up at specific times for particular events." But "varying degrees of spiritual amnesia" confront us when our spirit body reduces its vibration to match the energy of earth. We forget who we really are, parts of God in human form.

Samantha truly recognizes what she planned almost three years later while reading a paragraph in <u>For the Aspiring Mystic</u>.

"The desire to be loved is really the desire of the Spirit to love our world through us. As we consent to its action, the Spirit itself fulfills our desire. We experience the deep and abiding love that is the Spirit in us giving itself to itself in others and in our world. Eventually, our need to be loved by 'others' is diminished, for we directly experience divine love as it flows through us."

2. Samantha believes the course of life is preplanned so she could not have changed what happened to Daniel. No one else could have changed things either. It seems that the more lessons she learns in one life, the fewer lives she has to live. That, is the reason her soul chose a life of struggle, full of lessons to learn. Our free will can lessen or lengthen time on earth. It is up to us to learn the lessons that face us or to walk the other way. Samantha now feels Daniel's soul chose to sacrifice his life so others could learn lessons.

As Ernest Holmes tells us in <u>The Science of Mind</u>, man is free. Yet to become aware of his freedom, "he must first go through experiences which will teach him how to use his freedom properly."

Samantha's beliefs are now just as shattered as Daniel's body and motorcycle. And yet she knows, Daniel learned his life's lessons and is finally free. One of Daniel's favorite rock groups, Limp Biscuit, sings, "Life's a lesson, you learn it when you're through."

As noted in <u>Emmanuel's Book</u>: "You will stay until your task is done, until your lessons are learned. And then we will all begin again in some other dimension to create in the name of God."

3. Daniel makes it easier for everyone by dying as he does in a number of ways. He dies near a guardrail, on the grassy part of the highway, between Interstate lanes going north and south, right before a cemetery visible to traffic. No one has to identify the remains or bear the anguish of watching him slowly die. The highway soon undergoes construction and workers replace the guardrail with a concrete wall. Construction crew remove a roadside sign, which notes his passing, and later place it in two different spots making it more difficult to find. It now sits almost a quarter of a mile from where his body landed.

4. No one yet knows there are no accidents. Everything evolves around the Divine Laws of Love, Balance, Order, Cause, and Effect. As souls, we all choose what family to be born into and when the day and time of our birth will be. We create our life by what we choose to believe. And we choose when to leave the physical body. When a soul chooses to leave physicality it leaves despite earth ties.

5. Thoughts contribute greatly to experience. What we think about others is what we believe about our self, and what we do to others, we do to ourselves so it's vital to train our mind and consider only positive thoughts.

Thinking of anyone in a negative way is harmful for a mental medium exists between us. There are no idle thoughts. Mind Principle, Ernest Holmes wrote in <u>This Thing Called You</u>, is reactive to thought and very susceptible to *impression. It acts upon the slightest vibration of thought producing a corresponding thing.*

Yes, thinking produces form. What happens in life depends greatly on how powerful you know your thought to be and how you portray that thought. If you know your thoughts are powerful, and speak them with great intensity, they will manifest much more quickly. The Third Insight speaks of this dynamic energy noting that our thoughts influence other energy systems and increase the pace of coincidences in our lives.

It's vital to remember this is only a dream world. Problems show up as the ego's attempt to get you to react, to feel things such as guilt, and anger, separating you from other people. Once you give validity to the ego's world, you reinforce everything that seems to be around you.

Projection of guilt unto others is a way of escaping from unconscious guilt. The guilt we feel is really about our seeming separation from God, the One in which we live, and move, and have all BEing. There is no separation from the One. <u>A Course in Miracles</u> *explains:*

"Your other life has continued without interruption, and has been and always will be totally unaffected by your attempts to dissociate it."

All living things exist within the One. As a drop of ocean water is part of the ocean so too are we part of One.

It's vital to invalidate the ego. There is just one thing to do when we negatively react to what happens. We forgive our self for believing the contents of the ego mind and recognize Oneness with all people. Sometimes it helps at first to start by forgiving whoever you think has offended you for not knowing this is a dream world and there is just One.

:-)

~ 2 ~

Preparing for Change

Terrance, Samantha's brother, arrives as the women continue to cry in shock over Daniel's quick passing. Daniel and Terrance are only two-years apart in age. They grew up together as if brothers. Anger rears its ugly head. Daniel will never be bald and he won the family's game because he died with the most toys. By afternoon, James, Ruth, Terrance and Rebecca are anxious to see the accident site. They all pile into Ruth's black Chevy van for the drive.

The trip is not important to Samantha. She cannot bear the thought of actually looking at the spot on the highway where Daniel's body laid. Alone for the first time since hearing the news, another instant when she thought he was gone forever spurts forth. A quick look through journals finds the entry written in 1984.

"What causes me to write? It could be progress, regression, a need to view thoughts in retrospect, habit, or sheer loneliness. Maybe it's a combination of them all. In any event, I can't sleep. I toss and turn, remember my firstborn is trying his wings (the ones I've strived so hard to mold for him so he could face the world head on) and mourn for the emptiness I feel inside.

"It's hollow and cold, dark and sharp with pinpricks. I remember when Daniel was only a few months old and his father took him from me. I felt so empty then. I still felt the loss even with the sleeping pills I used to escape life. At least then, I should have known I'd get him back. This, now, is his choice and perhaps even mine. For him to view the world as it can be when one is not fully prepared for all its demands.

"Unless life plays yet another cruel trick on me, I'll be able to once again feel peaceful and content in the knowledge that I have armed him with the things he needs to live a fruitful and productive life.

"Actually, I handled his move quite well. Daniel kept looking at me as if to say, 'Well Mom, are you going to have your tantrum? Will you test your power over me or melt into a weepy puddle?' Although I may have appeared upset, I didn't break down until several hours after his final load was off the truck and placed inside the first residence of his own choosing.

"Maybe he was surprised and disappointed that I didn't beg him to stay. I let him know he could always move back home. He looked sincere when he said that was nice to know. I know it will never be the same. We will never relate to one another as we have in the past. Although that is good, I mourn for this child who I fought for and struggled to hold close to me for seventeen years. And that is good too."

Tears now flow down Samantha's face. Remembering that time, and comparing it to his death, leaves her no comfort. It occurs to her that having a friend, who lost her son years before, was meant to prepare her for the last loss of Daniel. Something then prompts her to watch family videos documenting how much Daniel learned over his human life.

Daniel became interested in Samantha's political emails three months before physical death. Sensing impending doom, Samantha constantly taped House and Senate hearings keeping track of the loss of democracy. Daniel thanked her for enlightening him on issues that he normally didn't focus on. He'd been trying to make a difference in the world but was disillusioned as well. Daniel felt his efforts would not change the ultimate outcome that people with money, and power, would control the world.

Samantha made plans for her own transition only two months before Daniel's death. She'd never thought that human life was easy. Over the past few years, something on her right side, near the middle of her upper chest, bothered her a great deal. It made her fat throat feel odd. She repeatedly burped with her mouth closed until she gasped for breath. The throat problem made it nearly impossible to take medications. Pills often broke apart in her throat causing it to burn, leaving a bitter taste in her mouth.

Every time she saw a doctor, they made another diagnosis, prescribed another pill, ordered another test, or suggested another surgery. Having finished taking steroids for osteoarthritis, without relief, doctors asked her to consider epidurals to relieve the constant pain. She refused the treatment not wanting to fill her body with more drugs.

Another doctor wanted her to have an invasive endoscopy and that was the last straw. She was unwilling to take the test not knowing if it would negatively affect her medication schedule and other medical conditions. Her heart, irritable bowel and bladder always bothered her more when under stress. The test would just be one more thing to upset the status quo that had taken her years to achieve.

Samantha signed a statement saying she did not want the test. She'd had enough of pain, enough limitations, enough drugs, and enough of not being able to do things most people her age could do. At 53-years-old, she had almost had enough of life, almost, but not quite yet.

Samantha was accustomed to change. She changed her name several times without knowing our frequency changes when we call ourselves by a different name. She was "Squeaky" in the late 60's because of laryngitis. During the early 70's, Shar was the name friends used, while in the late 70's, truck drivers at a waitress job referred to her as Sam. When she married James, her initials became SAM and by February 2002, most friends referred to her as Sam. She liked the nickname but had no idea that changing your name affects your way of life.

Samantha decided months ago that she had learned her life lessons. There were just a few more things to do. She wanted to spend more time with family to make up for missed time over the years due to her workaholic ways.

Paying for a prepaid cremation sounded good and she wanted to make a memorial CD of her favorite songs for the family.

In her mind, life was over but she wouldn't take back a single moment. There were few regrets, for she knew every experience brought her to where she was. Samantha knew she lived many lives and was now fed up and tired of living. It upset her that changes she thought necessary to help humankind were not apparent. Everyone seemed lost as lambs heading toward a slaughterhouse of limitation. Yet, she was no longer willing to change anything. [6]

Watching news stations every day brought fear to Samantha's mind. She sensed unwanted changes continuing to affect how people lived. As Daniel, she too felt helpless to change what was to come in the future. It seemed that more people were becoming fearful and ready to attack others before attack. More people were willing to give up personal freedom to be "protected" by government. [7]

Samantha feared that she'd become totally useless and a burden to her family. Although there were a few more things to accomplish, she was tired of limitations and ready to go on to her next life. Samantha was tired of taking medications that lessened the pain but helped her to be somewhat useful. They only served to decrease her quality of life even further.

Samantha told Rebecca her life force was getting weaker. She just didn't feel as committed to work as in the past. There was a nagging thought that she had to do something. But even with increased dosage for the hypothyroidism, she was tired all the time. She just wanted to sleep and never wake up.

Daniel, Samantha believed, found his way after years of struggle, so she wasn't too worried about him. Yet, it was important for her to know that Rebecca and Samuel would be okay after she died. Rebecca suffered from serious medical issues and had recently left her fiancé of eight years.

Having a premonition of impending doom, she wrote

a note to her family to read after she died. She told them death was a part of life but they would see each other again in a different life. Samantha sadly paid for her cremation depressed for those she'd leave behind. She paid the extra fee for international transportation of her remains even though she never traveled outside of the U.S. or Canada.

Back home, Samantha sorted through old record albums looking for music to record for her memorial CD. She wanted everyone to know she was finally happy because she died. Formatting *"In the Name of Love"* by Carole King onto the laptop computer was easy. But a strange thing happened when she listened to the song later. The speed of the music increased unexpectedly at the end. And now, after Daniel's untimely passing, she realized her dad's spirit was with her when she recorded it. And if he could be with her then, Daniel could be with her now.

6. Samantha didn't realize the true meaning of race consciousness. She had no idea that what the masses believe often manifests on the earth plane. Everything is part of the collective waveform of consciousness. Race beliefs and the thought-currents of our more immediate environment tend to affect what we think. The creative power of thought used in the wrong direction produces limitations. Thomas Troward noted humans "are subject to a very powerful negative influence" from those unaware of affirmative principles.

Ernest Holmes noted the "everywhere present" mental medium between humans in 1926. Individual mentalities are in sympathetic vibration with each other and can receive suggestions from one another. The accumulated mentality of humans living in different locations of the world serves to highlight why people have so many different beliefs. We choose where to direct our attention, and energy, and each level of awareness offers us an opportunity to expand our idea of existence.

As reported by Dr. Page:
"We exist in a holographic Universe which means

that it's as real as our mind perceives it to be. If you believe it, there is the potential to create it."

Daniel's spirit will soon lead Samantha to new atmospheres where she will open her mind. She will clearly hear an unknown voice while reading about race-suggestions.

"New souls are now being born because there are just too many jaded souls now."

7. Fear occurs when there is doubt and separation from the Self. Samantha, did not nourish her soul nor act from a place of wisdom. The daily struggle of trying to protect her own needs drove her further away from Truth. The Eternal Source of Power within us all remained elusive for Samantha found it hard to trust anyone, sometimes even herself. Fear, an addiction more powerful than most chemical drugs, kept Samantha from learning lessons throughout life. Dr. Page notes fear is like shame for it holds the key to a deeper level of emotion. If we have the courage to face it, we can release increasing quantities "of vital energy within ourselves in the name of excitement, enthusiasm and love of life." As noted by a wise Hawaiian Elder: "Fear always separates us from our true self and makes us vulnerable to the whims of others...."

Fear closes off the Light of God and separates humans from It. Renard notes that fear is one of the greatest denials of the reality of God. God, or pure Spirit, is the only true reality. Emmanuel notes fear is a cornerstone of the karmic condition. It's a distrust of Eternal Love, a disbelief in the self, and a perversion of Love, Truth, and Light. The world is all about healing these extreme distortions.

Many humans are now waking to the realization that there are merely two choices on this planet, fear or Love. Fear will cease to exist once the realization of our True Nature as Love becomes widespread.

:-)

~ 3 ~
Sherman's Ultimate Gift

A car accident fatally injured Sherman, Samantha's father, less than two years before Daniel's transition. She was still struggling with his loss for they had not been very close. The way he died disturbed her greatly. Seeing the way he lived before his death was equally disturbing.

Sherman wanted his first child to be a boy. As the first-born child, Samantha didn't like being with him and refused to go fishing. She now thought about how his death was part of 'the plan.' Sherman's accident occurred in Michigan, on a Friday, two weeks before Thanksgiving.

Most of the family planned to enjoy a weekend trip to Florida's West coast to experience the "Mystery Train Dinner Theatre." Everyone was excited and looked forward to the work break for several months. It was a time to reconnect and strengthen family bonds in a relaxing atmosphere of leisure and fun. Samantha was packing her suitcase when she answered the persistent ringing telephone.

"Dad's in the hospital Samantha," her brother Aaron in Detroit, Michigan said. "The hospital just called and said he was in a car accident."

She sat down in shock. Most people referred to Aaron as the "slow child" when they were growing up. He now knew only the name of the hospital that cared for Sherman. The hospital wouldn't give Samantha any information over the telephone.

Their parents divorced years ago so Sherman was no longer a part of their lives. Last year however, Ruth, who was usually careful not to spend money, acted on a hunch and surprised everyone. She paid to fly Sherman, Aaron, and Aaron's wife Matilda to South Florida for the Christmas holiday.

If the rest of Sherman's family needed to go to Detroit, they'd need to make travel arrangements and plan time off from work. It was too much to think about for Samantha. She phoned Ruth to discuss when to tell everyone. Ruth and Samantha chose to wait until the end of everyone's workday so they could make a decision together. They knew so little about the accident and when the rest of the family heard the news, it was hard to decide what to do. Daniel was the first to ask, "When do we leave Mom?"

They decided to continue with the Fort Myers trip until they learned more about Sherman's condition. Daniel agreed to contact Aaron later since he and Rachel weren't joining the rest of the family until the next night. They knew Aaron would know more about the accident after he got to the hospital.

Ruth, Terrance, James, and Samantha drove with dread across Alligator Alley to Fort Myers. Rebecca couldn't get time off from work. A ten to twelve hour day job as a restaurant manager kept her too busy to enjoy herself.

Later that night, Daniel telephoned the family with his report. A truck backed quickly down a driveway into Sherman's car as he drove along a busy street. Aaron told him there was now a tube down Sherman's throat. Feeling nauseous, and somewhat sorry for learning so much by working in hospitals, Samantha was the only one who recognized the dubious sign. Her dad was now on a ventilator that helped him breathe. He could not breathe on his own. Aaron said he arrived at the hospital before doctors placed the tube.

Sherman told him, "Sue the bastards."

They laughed thinking it true to Sherman's form for he'd started many unsuccessful lawsuits. Daniel then announced a change in his plans. Joy changed her mind and would not be watching 11-month-old Abigail during their thirty-six hour weekend. The baby was coming with them to experience the "Mystery Train Dinner Theatre."

Everyone decided to take turns telephoning Aaron for updates until they learned the full extent of Sherman's condition. Rebecca offered to phone him from work, and try to telephone the hospital, to see if she could rope an unsuspecting nurse into giving out more information. Samantha called the hospital to ask for her father's room number. Later, she decided that the night nurses were not as busy and might offer much needed information. She made several telephone calls after midnight and finally got through to the Intensive Care Unit's (ICU) Nurse's Station. The nurse told her only that her father's condition was the same as the day before.

Sherman might want to see them and they wanted to be there for him, and for Aaron. Since they wanted to go to Michigan, but needed to get the time off work, they were already making plans. Samantha began to telephone the airlines as Daniel, Rachel, and baby Abigail drove across Alligator Alley on that sunny Saturday to be with the rest of the family. It was lunchtime when they arrived. Rachel's hazel eyes looked sad as she wiped her long blonde hair away from her face for Daniel's kiss. The rest of the family left to find a public place to use computers while Rachel settled in with Abigail at the hotel.

Rebecca arranged for a rental car from her home computer while Samantha made airline and hotel reservations on a computer at a Fort Myer's Kinko's. They both wondered what they'd do without charge cards. Daniel and Ruth frantically telephoned their bosses to get time off work. Terrance went from one family member to the other reporting their progress.

Samantha telephoned Aaron to report that they'd join him soon. She knew he wouldn't know what to do. With an overwhelming feeling of dread in her gut, she telephoned the hospital again. She wanted to ask Sherman's nurse to tell him his children in Florida were coming on Monday. She knew if on the verge of death, the knowledge of their visit would keep him alive, until they got there to say goodbye. A knowledgeable ICU nurse admitted Sherman's condition was serious. She thought Sherman would still be alive when they got there. Samantha felt like a warrior coming back from battle, weary, but joyful, because she'd succeeded in getting a message to her father.

Knowing they couldn't leave for Michigan for two more days they reluctantly got ready to board the dinner train. They needed the time on the train to pull themselves together as a family. Rachel reluctantly stayed at the hotel with Abigail because the dinner show people didn't want small children there. They were afraid that a baby might disrupt the experience of the adults who paid more than $50 each to be there.

The rest of the family trudged onto the train. It was extremely difficult to pay attention to the show because they kept speculating as to exactly how bad Sherman's condition really was. Even though their alcoholic drinks were costly, they sopped up liquor like alcoholics. They were all drunk and happy that the hotel was only blocks away by the time the train arrived back at the small station.

All of them were bone weary tired. Samantha felt like she'd been beaten with sticks as she and James headed to their room. She left the room after a few minutes to get some ice just as Rachel came out into the hallway. Rachel appeared furious as she cradled Abigail in her arms. She saw Samantha and told her how very angry she was because she could not go to Michigan with Abigail. Rachel then implored Samantha to tell Daniel that Sherman would want to see his great granddaughter. Samantha thought differently, and again, felt an all too familiar pain in her heart along with a feeling of dread in her gut.

"He's never seen her," Rachel yelled as they stood in the hotel corridor.

Baby Abigail began to cry. Samantha was heart sick at the thought of such a fury of feelings for everyone. Hotel room doors quickly opened, and slowly shut, when the other guests saw what was taking place.

Samantha tried without success to explain that the only time babies were in a hospital was when they were born or sick. She knew it was out of the question to reason with Rachel. Rachel's voice rose as she stepped towards Samantha menacingly and the 'fight' escalated. Samantha wondered if Rachel was going to chase her down the hall as she had chased Rebecca down the street trying to hit her one sad Fourth of July.

Abigail clung to Rachel crying and looking scared. Huge crocodile tears streamed down her tiny, heart-shaped face but Rachel seemed unaware of Abigail's distress. Daniel came out of their room, stood between Rachel and Samantha, and waved Samantha calmly towards her room. She thankfully joined James who was totally unaware of what happened. The television blared loudly in the adjoining room as Ruth and Terrance watched a comedy show.

The next morning, Daniel brought Abigail down for breakfast while Rachel stayed in the room. He calmly asked Samantha to change his flight reservations so he could return home two days sooner. Although he said his boss needed him back at work earlier, she didn't believe it. He promised to meet Ruth, Rebecca, Terrance, and Samantha at the airport on Monday morning before trudging back to his hotel room to pack.

Ruth coughed and Samantha wondered if she too was fighting back tears. It hurt her to see Daniel looking so defeated but now it was a sadly familiar hurt. Daniel, Rachel and Abigail soon left for home. They followed his route an hour later. A sense of doom filled the van as they drove silently past the Indian Reservation and through the Everglades.

:-)

~ 4 ~

Daddy Wins the Lotto

Daniel, Ruth, Rebecca, Terrance, and Samantha, flew to Michigan on Spirit Airlines Monday, November 18, at 6:30 AM, after hurriedly packing the night before. Ruth was coughing more and feeling like she had the beginning of the flu.

Frigid air surrounded them outside the Detroit airport. They all shook like alcoholics, coming off from a binge, even though they wore their Detroit winter clothes. The walk to the rental car agency, where the bus drove them to a Sports Utility Vehicle (SUV), was short but enough to warm them.

Rebecca and Daniel appeared strong while mentally supporting the older adults. Samantha was proud to see her two kids acting like grownups. Rebecca signed for the beautiful limited edition cruiser and Daniel took on the responsibility of driving. They were the threads that held the family together when the others lost their composure. After checking in at a two-bedroom apartment to drop off their luggage, they all went to see Sherman.

It was a shock to see Sherman, helpless in critical condition, wearing a neck collar. Numerous tubes, seeming to emit from every hole in his body, surrounded him. Monitors showed his slow but steady heartbeat, blood pressure, and respirations. The ventilator hissed as Samantha watched fluid move through a tube from his stomach to the receptacle that collected waste. Bloodstained urine left his body and flowed into another waste container.

Sherman seemed totally unaware of their presence. His 5' 8" frame weighed several pounds more and his stomach looked huge. Most of his thin silver hair was gone. The hospital had shaved away his rough-looking beard but his mustache remained. Sherman's rotted teeth, stained from years of chewing tobacco, surrounded the tube down his throat.

Samantha quickly realized her dad was dying as she watched the red colored urine leave his body. She was silently thankful for the talk they had the previous Christmas. Sherman, with tears in his eyes, stopped her in the hall as she walked by the food pantry. He then apologized for his actions when his children were growing up. It was uncomfortable for them both as Sherman started to cry. Samantha was shocked to see his tears and, despite his strong body odor, gave him a hearty hug.

"Daddy, no one gets an instruction book when they have kids," she announced. "We all just do the best we can and learn along the way."

Sherman seemed comforted and went back to sit alone on the living room sofa.

Samantha's focus changed when the nurse entered the room. He soon advised them to call the specialist that admitted Sherman to the hospital. Aaron arrived but didn't know any more than they did. Samantha quickly called her best friend Esther, a Registered Nurse, to ask if she had friends at the hospital that might help them learn more about Sherman's condition. Esther agreed to see them on her lunch hour the next day.

Esther and Samantha met while both in their twenties struggling through bad marriages. Their sporadically employed husbands rode motorcycles and both women had young daughters, a year apart in age. They helped one another through many trouble-filled days during their twenty-seven year friendship. The distance in miles made no difference for they still helped each other when they could.

The family spent a few hours staring mindlessly at Sherman. They left the hospital that night without seeing any doctors.

Daniel drove through a restaurant drive-through to make sure everyone ate. Their daily planning process began while eating back at the apartment. Ruth was really sick by this time and unable to talk. The guilt she felt toward her dad was strong. Daniel and Rebecca remained steady, caring, compassionate, and patient rocks, with positive attitudes, that helped the family deal with their pain throughout heaps of daily tasks.

On Tuesday, and each morning for the rest of the week, they called Aaron to coordinate the day's travel. Aaron's disabled wife, Matilda, confined to a wheelchair, was unable to help. Doctors found her brain tumor early, a month after they married. A stroke during surgery left her paralyzed, even after years of therapy. Yet, Aaron remained devoted to his morbidly obese, red-haired wife.

Six doctors now cared for Sherman. His new neck collar was hard to miss when the family got to the hospital. Esther soon stopped by to give hugs and emotional support. Her opinion mattered a great deal to thankful Samantha. Sadly, but with assurety of mind, Esther told them Sherman's situation appeared bleak and they needed to think about what to do. They thanked her and she returned to her hospital job a few miles away.

Sherman slowly opened his eyes after Esther left. Samantha could sense he wanted to die in peace and longed to see his dad, mom, sister and brothers. His eyes sparkled with delight as he saw most of his children and two grandchildren near his face. Samantha knew he felt like a big lottery winner with most of his family gathered around him.

Sherman looked into Samantha's eyes. She heard him inside her head ask about their mother. She told him mother wanted to come, and still loved him, but they just couldn't deal with her too. Their mom, diagnosed with schizophrenia many years ago, sometimes didn't understand what was happening around her. Although she divorced Sherman more than ten years earlier, they still loved one another.

Sherman appeared to understand and closed his eyes as if it was a great effort to keep them open. Samantha's cheeks began to redden as her blood pressure rose. She told the family it was time to say goodbye. One by one, they took turns talking to Sherman privately as the others stood in the cold, hospital hallway.

When it was Samantha's time, she went in and kissed his cheek. As she looked into her dad's eyes, she knew he was asking for forgiveness. He wanted his children to forgive him for not being what most people would refer to as a good father.

"We forgive you Daddy," she said with tears in her eyes. "It's okay. You can let go now."

His eyes closed and she sensed that he relaxed. [8]

The first doctor who saw Sherman then tells the family he was reluctant to use the ventilator. Sherman didn't want to be kept alive artificially. He said he had "lazy kidneys" but was in good health, he didn't drink, and wasn't on any medications. Samantha knew better but didn't dispute the information.

"There's something else going on," Dr. Tamara noted as if in heavy thought, "but we don't know what. He has a strange paralysis. There may be internal injuries."

Each day, doctors ordered more treatments and tests for Sherman. One ordered total parenteral nutrition (expensive nutritional therapy). The family had no idea what to do. They remained totally drained of energy after numerous trips to the hospital and to Aaron's house. Their hectic schedule included visits to grocery stores, restaurants, and the towing company. A trip to the police station to talk with the reporting officer led them to the most exhausting trip of all, the junk yard where Sherman's car now sat.

They saw the car early Wednesday morning. Daniel, Rebecca and Samantha felt Sherman's presence but they didn't say anything to the others. Aaron and Terrance wanted lots of pictures for evidence. Terrance had stayed closer to his dad since his son Joel was the only grandchild Sherman saw after most of the family moved. Sherman spent more time with Aaron after Terrance moved his small family and mother to South Florida.

A camera's film, notes Monroe in *Far Journeys*, sees light frequencies our eyes cannot. Samantha had no doubt that digital cameras pick up those frequencies. (Later, when she put the pictures on her home computer patches of white mist inside the car revealed that Sherman had indeed been with them in spirit form.)

Sherman's fever was "somewhat" down when they returned to the hospital. He was breathing more on his own. It was now a heart-wrenching situation for Sherman did not have a Living Will and could only move his eyes. The Infectious Disease Specialist told them on Thursday that Sherman's oxygen rate was improving but he had pneumonia so the doctors ordered more antibiotics. Doctors needed more blood tests to monitor his condition.

The family could do nothing but keep him connected to life-saving machines. They sat or stood near his bed and watched as black floaters glided slowly through Sherman's breathing tube into the collection container. Later, an Intern told them Sherman's kidney function was decreasing. He also had Staphylococcal Aureus, a severe blood infection, a fatty liver, and his heart was beginning to weaken. His skin was breaking down as well.

Sherman's kidneys began to fail. A doctor finally told them much later in the day that Sherman's spine damage was due to a bone spur in his neck. His prognosis was dim. The spur sliced through his spine during the accident and only a thread of it was connected. Even if other conditions improved, he would still be paralyzed.

    A wise male nurse then tried to help the family make a decision about his care. He decreased Sherman's morphine drip thinking it would help them to communicate with Sherman. Samantha stood as close as she could to her dad. She realized, for the first time, that his eyes were a brilliant shade of blue.

    Samantha knew her dad could hear. Looking into his eyes, she slowly asked him to tell her if he felt any pain. She asked him to blink his eyes twice if he did. Sherman managed to blink his blue eyes once but could not fully blink them again. She immediately had the nurse give him more morphine because she could not bear to see him suffer needlessly.

    Two doctors entered the room to talk about hooking Sherman up to a dialysis machine. His family left quickly to discuss his condition in the family waiting room. No one wanted Sherman to continue suffering. They quickly decided to stop the doctors from ordering additional treatments such as dialysis. Daniel then helped Samantha to convince the rest of the family it was time to let Sherman go. Everyone agreed that Samantha would sign a Do Not Resuscitate (DNR) order. After more talking, they agreed to order the hospital staff to "pull the plug," to disconnect the machine keeping Sherman alive. Samantha hurried to the Nurse's Station to announce her family's decision and quickly signed the order for the hospital staff to disconnect the ventilator.

    Evidence of yet another treatment became apparent upon returning to Sherman's room. Both legs were wrapped and connected to a machine to keep his blood circulating. Doctor's now noted he had no arm movement but, oddly, limited movement in one leg. There was no improvement in his condition as the family waited for several members of the hospital staff. But it was now time for Daniel to return home. Samantha, thankful that he was always the patient one in the family, knew he'd be missed. A brilliant shade of red again filled her cheeks as she kissed him goodbye. He drove the SUV to the airport with Terrance and Rebecca.

Ruth, feeling better, moved closer to her dad. Her voice was hoarse but at least she could now talk. She whispered to Sherman as Samantha stood in the hallway missing Daniel's positive attitude.

The room filled with hospital staff several hours later. As they began to turn off the ventilator, Aaron stopped them.

"Wait," he said anxiously, "maybe he doesn't want to die."

The health care team left the room immediately in silence.

"Let us know when you're all in agreement," the nurse announced softly before closing the door.

The family looked at Aaron in shock. Terrance, Ruth, and Rebecca took him into the family waiting room to review everything they knew again. Samantha was angry with Aaron and stayed to talk to Sherman. She didn't know if he heard her but she talked to him anyway not caring. Her face was now beefy red as she told him it was okay to go Home.

"You can go Home now Daddy and see Grandma and Grandpa," she said filled with determination.

The rest of the family came back to the room and again agreed to let Sherman die. Samantha went to the Nurse's Station with the news. The nurse at the desk told her she would relay the family's decision to the doctors. A full staff would need to be in the room to disconnect the machines. Sherman had to wait one more day to die.

Doctors again confirmed Sherman's condition the next morning. The accident caused a "partial severance of the spine." Even if Sherman recovered from secondary complications such as infection, pneumonia, and failing kidneys, he would still be paralyzed and unable to breathe on his own. The family knew their decision to "pull the plug" was the right thing to do.

Several doctors and other hospital staff entered the

room at 3:10 PM. One by one, they turned off a machine and left the room after doing their job. The heart monitor remained on but the alarm went off when the flat line appeared on its display screen. Sherman's family began to cry and the nurse went to stand outside the room.

Samantha watched and knew her father's death was very painful. For family members with medical conditions, worsened by stress, the experience was close to what she thought hell must be like. Yet, even though the week was traumatic for his family, watching his organs fail one by one, Sherman took the brunt of the pain. She had no idea that seeing him die would make a big difference in how she thought about death in the future.

Suddenly, the heart monitor began to beep as the line rose on the machine. The family stared at Sherman with disbelief. Maybe Sherman didn't want to die. Perhaps he would have a miracle recovery. The alarm then sounded as the flat line appeared again on his heart monitor. Within seconds, the monitor once again began to beep as if Sherman's heart was beating.

The nurse came into the room when the heart monitor seemed to come alive the third time. He unplugged the machine and said it was common for it to act as it had. Sherman was clinically dead. They cried with relief but all of them felt totally drained of life. Aaron returned home to Matilda, as Ruth, Rebecca, Terrance, and Samantha left for the rented apartment. They fell quickly asleep exhausted from their ordeal.

Tasks associated with Sherman's passing were discussed the next morning. Samantha listed the chores as the family talked about what to do. Sherman hadn't planned for his funeral, even though their mother told him, many times, not to leave it up to his kids. His assets included a little more than $400 in the bank and $6,000 in life insurance policies that named his boys as beneficiaries.

The list seemed endless as Samantha wrote down

each chore. Sherman had nothing of value in his rented trailer. The cost of his death was now a big concern. They needed to shut off utilities and contact his landlord. Someone had to give the junk yard the title to his totaled car to avoid the towing cost. There were funeral arrangements to make and relatives to notify. Everyone agreed to do something.

After little discussion, they decided not to have a service for Sherman. Ruth telephoned the crematorium to pick up Sherman's body from the hospital morgue. She put the cost of his cremation on one of her charge cards. No one possessed the energy, or will, to notify or visit relatives or friends. They all felt weak, totally drained of energy.

Terrance called the newspaper to print the death notice with as little information as possible. Ruth, Rebecca, and Samantha, having charged expenses for the past week, were now in debt. Neither Aaron nor Terrance had any money or even a credit card. No one but Aaron knew Daniel gave him $500 to cover unexpected expenses before he left.

Ruth, Rebecca, Terrance, and Samantha drove to Aaron and Matilda's house that Friday. Aaron planned to take them and Matilda's grown son out to an early dinner. The bleak landscape fit their mood as they drove. Dead tree leaves clung to bare branches. Some of the brown leaves sat on the ground in the white snow.

Samantha realized Aaron lived across the street from a cemetery stone-making business when they pulled into his driveway. The dark house felt oppressive so she was the first one to go back outside into the cold.

They ate quickly at the restaurant and then went to see their Aunt Lois. She'd waited expectantly for them the night before and told them the cousins and their spouses had waited too. They apologized for not coming or even remembering to call her. Aunt Lois and Cousin Olivia listened to what Sherman experienced as they all drank beer.

On Saturday, they went to clean out Sherman's trailer. The movie, "8-Mile," about the white rapper from

Detroit, was filmed in the trailer park where Sherman lived. Sherman had excitedly told them the film crew moved him out of his trailer and put him in a better one after the movie wrapped.

Samantha was horrified to see the limitation her father had chosen to accept. She thought Sherman must have lied. Maybe, the trailer park people changed their minds, because she could not imagine a trailer in worse shape than his. It smelled so bad that she gagged and could not even step inside. Stray cats, Sherman's only companions, came in and out through several holes in the bottom of the trailer.

Ruth, Aaron, and Terrance ventured inside as Samantha stood outside holding the door open. The trailer was devoid of human value except for family pictures Samantha sent Sherman throughout the years. They were scattered all around the place. Terrance and Aaron took some of Sherman's clothes and personal things but there wasn't much to take. Ruth gathered papers that she thought might be important. They handed everything to Rebecca and she loaded them into the rented SUV. Aaron and Matilda's garage served as a storage unit that evening.

After everyone looked through Sherman's papers on Sunday morning, Ruth started the paperwork to claim life insurance for Terrance, Aaron, and Amos. She then telephoned the Veteran's Administration so the government would recognize Sherman's service in World War II with a flag.

Aaron was adamant about suing the driver and the business he worked for so they discussed what to do about getting a lawyer. They decided Samantha would find one, for it seemed an easy thing to do, since she had Internet access and was more familiar with business people.

Samantha called the Social Security office so their mother could have her monthly check increased. Momma had repeatedly said she would be happy when Sherman died so she could collect his benefits. Samantha wondered why she could not collect them before he died for their marriage lasted more than thirty years. Her mom then lost some medical benefits because she got a few hundred dollars more per month. It was a lesson for the whole family to be careful with wishes.

Aaron was left with the task of taking care of the rest of Sherman's business, including his address change and dealing with the property owner. He went back to his dad's trailer after Ruth, Rebecca, Terrance, and Samantha returned home. Aaron knew the many stray cats were important to Sherman so he wanted to care for them. He also thoroughly cleaned and sanitized the trailer because he was embarrassed to let anyone see the way Sherman lived.

He closed Sherman's bank account and paid some bills, including the cost of the ambulance to the hospital. Later, Aaron paid the rest of the bills with some of the life insurance money that he got. Terrance paid his own bills and their oldest brother Amos, a long-term addict, used his money for crack.

Amos was the favored child, the fourth live child to come out of his mother's womb and their first son. The day after he married, he lost his temper and hit his wife. She left and never returned. The thought of losing her and his newborn daughter was too much to bear. He used drugs in his teens and moved on to cocaine. When the cocaine wasn't enough to get him high he started using crack.

Samantha was ashamed and saddened by not knowing how poorly her father lived in his final years alone. She felt he punished himself for things did before losing his family. Although they all felt totally drained of energy, Samantha knew there was a reason for it all. She just had no idea what it was at the time. [9]

8. Samantha would feel guilt later because she did not ask Sherman to forgive her for ignoring his important role in her soul's growth. She snubbed him for many years, only communicating during the last five years of his life. Ruth made it possible for her to reconnect with him on Christmas the year before. Samantha was thankful she had a few moments alone with him then.

While reading about the studies of Japanese scientist, Masuro Emoto, Samantha would realize how detrimental or positive words could be. Emoto showed, in graphic form, that words change the structure of water by reorganizing it around minerals and the vibration of words and thoughts. Dr. Page notes in <u>Spiritual Alchemy</u>, "Imagine the effects of words repeated several times a day on someone's crystalline cellular structure and especially on the delicately balanced immune system. **Words and thoughts have power; use them wisely.**"

Samantha wished she had asked her dad to forgive all of his children. She knew his visit during the Christmas holidays was not pleasant. Negative words flowed between him and family. She learned about these interactions after he went back to Michigan. Yet, the strain between other family members prompted him to talk with Samantha on Christmas day.

Now she knew there was nothing to forgive. This life is a dream in an illusory world and we must wake-up to Reality. Each one of us must forgive others and ourselves for even thinking we are not still one with God. As noted in <u>Spiritual Alchemy</u>, "...true forgiveness occurs not in the head as an idea but on a psychocellular level which can never be undone."

Souls choosing to be attached to lifesaving machines, Van Praagh reports, may help science for future generations, or assist family members. Sherman's soul chose to help his family, as he remained attached to the machines that kept him alive. There were lessons to learn of love, receiving love, compassion, and appreciating the sanctity of life.

Since Sherman was an atheist, it was vitally important for him to pass astutely, surrounded by loving family. Being aware of love and forgiveness, in his drugged state, he knew what he needed to do was ask for forgiveness. Yet, he wasn't asking for the forgiveness of his children. He was asking God to forgive him because he hadn't realized there is only One. There is no separation for there is only One in which we live.

Although he was not enlightened, Sherman's mind-body knew it was time to go Home. Sherman sought the forgiveness of God as his soul recognized the One within. The drugs helped still his mind to the point where he could hear his soul, where he could hear the God within. And he knew that his life as an atheist was a choice. That choice molded not only his life but the life of his children as well.

It was a choice his father made and his father had not died astutely. His father died alone in a hospital bed cringing and fighting dark figures. And yet, knowing that it's just a dream and thoughts are things, there really are no dark forces. There is One, one Light, one Truth, one Love, one BEing in which we all live, and move, and have all BEing. It is the Eternal Light of God flowing unerringly within all living things.

9. Sherman's family members needed to learn what someone with his conditions looked like. Keeping their soul agreements, they learned lessons of love, compassion, and the sanctity of human life. And they were all there to prepare for Daniel's upcoming death. Samantha's experience included lessons about limitation. She realized later that her dad's soul chose how to transition before he was born. He agreed to help his family learn valuable lessons as his mind-body seemed to suffer. In return, they helped Sherman's soul to astutely leave, surrounded by love, when the mind-body finally died.

Samantha was very clear on this point five years later, after reading <u>Dying to Live Again-Channeled Interviews with Souls from the Otherside</u> by Sally Baldwin. Upon entering human form, Sally notes, we are aware of the exquisite experience of merging back within the One when *the mind-body dies. The love, peace, and joy felt by the soul at this time is unmatched by any other experience, on any plane. "Souls need not be so excited about body, mind and ego and need to feel the astute energy now. The earth is so badly in need of astute energy of the soul."*

Feeling this energy we are more likely to understand who we are as souls, individualized parts of God.

Everything that happened after Sherman's death was preplanned as well. Daniel would have been confined in the same vegetative state if he chose to live after his own accident. He was there to help Sherman pass over to the Otherside and helped the family reason with Aaron so Sherman's soul could leave astutely.

Samantha soon sensed that both Sherman and James's father, Zephaniah, met Daniel when it was his time to pass over to the Otherside. Yet, she still didn't know how much her parent's had taught her. Without their human knowledge, or her own, she was now learning how to break the energy patterns that never fed their souls.

Samantha's soul chose her parents because they allowed her soul the freedom it needed to grow. Sherman taught Samantha valuable lessons, such as self-reliance, that helped her to break her soul's cycle of limitation and bondage. She learned to take care of herself and her family because he was irresponsible. Samantha's early struggles to survive made her strong. She knew what it was like to have people laugh at her because she wore rags. And she learned how to live without electricity, running water, or a steady food supply.

While her mother babysat for other families, Samantha helped to care for her sisters and brothers before she was five-years-old. Ruth and Samantha learned, at a very early age, how to make money to buy food. They climbed people's fruit trees and sold the fruit door to door. And at 15-years-old, Samantha started a family of her own.

Armed with lessons of love, learned from her mother,

and responsibility learned from her father, she was now the family's role model. Her personal strength helped her and her family through many tough times but she still had a lot to learn. She was nearly forty years of age before she knew that every second of life on earth is precious. Time shouldn't be wasted on "small stuff" and yes, everything on earth is "small stuff."

:-)

~ 5 ~

The Nightmare Continues

Thoughts turn to Daniel as Samantha sits in the brown, leather Lazy Boy with closed eyes. She remembers his lifelong love of motorcycles. His father, Peter, bought one to build shortly after Daniel's birth but since the parts remained scattered, he rode other people's bikes. Aunt Ruth taught Daniel to ride her motorcycle well before he got his driver's license. Samantha smiles upon remembering Daniel working on his first moped at 16-years-old. Suddenly, she hears his voice.

"It was a temporary lapse of judgment Mom. I was going 140 miles an hour."

Tears again flow like a river down her cheeks. She telephones Rachel when she can cry no more. It sounds as if Rachel and Joy are playing the same blame game that continues at Samantha's house. They speak of suing the driver of the car Daniel hit, thinking they might have been racing, and the car subsequently cut him off. It makes no difference to Samantha.

"Daniel always wanted to die while riding his motorcycle," she replies softly before asking to help with his arrangements. Rachel listens intently as she explains how 11-year-old Daniel signed, and witnessed, her wishes for cremation upon death as she prepared for her third surgery. Daniel then told everyone he wanted cremation too. He continued to remind his family that he didn't want his body to be buried in the ground. Daniel, Samantha notes, didn't want a funeral but a big celebration of life party. He wants everyone to rejoice in the fullness of his life and remember him as a free spirit. Daniel wants everyone to have a good time. [10]

Rachel listens to Samantha's suggestions and

promises to relay Daniel's arrangements. Samantha ends the call feeling helpless and again breaks out into sobs. Two hours later, with parts from Daniel's motorcycle, the family returns to find her still sitting in the Lazy Boy.

Rachel, Abigail, and Joy share their grief the next day. Samantha tearfully removes a small blackboard and chalk from the pantry. The blackboard holds smiley faces from two weeks before when Abigail learned how to draw them. Daniel had come to pick Abigail up and gladly joined them on the floor to draw that day.

Daniel and Samantha shared a special attraction to the sun and smiley faces reminded them of it. She called him her sunshine boy, since his birth, even though the first few years of his life were turbulent in many ways.

Samantha now recalls how two-year-old Abigail laughed at Daniel as he drew his first big smiley face. He made the face different from the way Samantha did, with big circles for eyes instead of little dots.

"That's not the way to make them Daddy," Abigail said. As Daniel drew another face she put her small hands on her hips, raised her voice insistently and said, "You're not doing it right Daddy."

Daniel looked perplexed until Samantha explained it was easier for his two-year-old to draw dots instead of circles for eyes. He laughed while making big smiley faces easier for her to draw.

"I never knew there was so much to having a child," he said pulling Abigail happily onto his lap.

Abigail now looks confused upon seeing the blackboard.

Samantha points to

the big smiley face Daniel made. She wants Abigail to know that her daddy is happy and wants her to be happy. Quiet Abigail puts her hand in her mouth. Samantha again tries to show her how to draw smiley faces but Abigail turns and points, as if seeing something no one else can see. Rachel, Abigail, and Joy leave hurriedly minutes later.

Many people besides Samantha clearly seem to feel guilt after Daniel's death. Samantha believes it's meant to be that way. As difficult as it seems, it's time to carry on and put the past behind her. She suspects that she's living in a nightmare dream world and there's no way out.

Family and friends hear the news of Daniel's departure from Rebecca and Ruth while Samantha deals with grief. Since she can't talk to anyone about his death, Samantha types feelings into a computer. Rebecca composes her brother's obituary, telephones the local newspaper to read the obituary out loud, and puts the cost on her charge card with tear-filled eyes.

The undisputed facts are clear. Daniel was on the way home to Rachel and Abigail before the accident. He flipped up over his bike to land near the middle of Interstate 95, when the cycle's front wheel hit the rear, driver side of the car in front of him. Daniel's neck broke and he had many other injuries. Blood tests show he was beyond the legal limit for alcohol. They also found prescription painkillers in his blood system.

It was after midnight, before the time change, on April 4, 2004. The date meant something to Samantha later upon hearing that the number four is a reference to God and Oneness. A chance meeting with another conference attendee four years later gives her much needed information. The stranger notes God uses the number three to get people's attention and the number four refers to creation. Samantha saw the numbers in many places but they didn't prompt her to think of God who then walloped her with a bunch of fours.

Now, as one of her molars begins to throb, she

suddenly knows, Daniel's death was her soul's planned wake-up call. Since she hadn't listened to God, the triple four was a slap in the face. A picture of Samuel at two-years-old, proudly holding two playing cards for Nana to see surprises her. The cards are the numbers three and four. God works through all humans and children are our best teachers.

    The disputed truth is that Daniel and the driver of the car he hit were speeding, perhaps racing one another. Daniel may have tried to pass the car and misjudged the distance. Some family members join Rachel and Joy in believing that the driver of the car cut him off from winning the race.

    Samantha, on the cusp of sleep while still in the Lazy Boy, now hears Daniel's voice. Yes, he drove by to see her on his way home that night. She quickly recognizes this truth for Daniel knew she didn't sleep until 3:00 AM. She was unusually tired before midnight on that particular night. It seemed as if she was in some kind of a trance as she sat in the Lazy Boy. Exhausted, she reached up to turn down the living room light, three hours earlier than usual, making it hard to see the light on from outside the house.

    A motorcycle drove by moments later as Samantha hovered on the cusp of sleep. "If it's Daniel," she thought, "he will stop to see me." She had not seen the fast, red motorcycle purchased for his thirty-seventh birthday less than two months before. The motorcycle drove away after a very short hesitation. "It can't be him," she thought drifting off to sleep, "I know he would stop to see me."

    Upon reading *The Afterlife Experiments* by Gary Schwartz months later, a new dimension of reality would appear and she'd know that his energy consciousness would remain part of her life.

    10. Daniel was cremated after his funeral and later Samantha would discover why they always wanted cremation with a scattering of ashes. Dr. Page notes:

    "Air reconnects us to our Source by assisting us in releasing archaic bonds to people and attitudes... Although

all the elements are involved in the grief process, air's only concern is to return us to spirit."

There's a powerful effect of "scattering ashes" after a cremation and burning memories that are no longer part of history. In simpler terms, Van Praagh notes, cremation is especially vital in cases "of suicide or a tragic accident." If the spirit is still in an earthbound state, it feels physical ties that hinder the soul from becoming aware of its new situation.

Despite cremation, Daniel will keep physical ties to earth, until he takes care of unfinished business. Samantha will quickly learn to help his spirit free itself in the months ahead. Rachel will bear the burden of keeping Daniel's ashes. And the accident site will become the place where family and friends, who refer to him as DOG, go to pass time with him. Their cars, vans, and trucks will park in the median between the highway lanes as they leave memories and write farewells on the guardrail.

Samantha will feel a certain satisfaction in reading about physical death years later in several books. Emmanuel notes dying is an exciting entrance instead of an exit. Death is like finally taking off a stuffy business suit to replace it with comfortable leisure clothes. It is of Divine origin and the process is always joyous once the fear of death is gone.

Elizabeth Kubler-Ross reminds us, "There are no mistakes, no coincidences, all events are blessings given to us to learn from."

Learning lessons chosen in each life guides us back to our True Source. The illusory death of physical bodies is a graduation day, a celebration because it means we have learned our lessons. This experience allows us to go through a much greater version of life, another level of more intense existence. We are released to reconstruct "the image of Self into the Oneness of all things" without losing the Self.

Edgar Cayce also believed soul growth depended on learning spiritual lessons. He noted three keys to soul growth: setting spiritual ideas; applying spiritual principles on earth; and personal attunement with the Divine.

:-)

~ 6 ~
Shock City

Samantha's toothache is a blessing in disguise for pain often steals time. The painful tooth is one filled with metal during the year of Daniel's birth. It now throbs constantly forcing her to visit the family dentist. X-rays reveal nothing that would cause her pain. The general dentist prescribes painkillers and arranges an appointment with a dental specialist.

County medical examiners autopsy Daniel's body because his death is an accident. The body is ready for viewing at the funeral home three days later. But Samantha refuses to go. Sedated by painkillers, she seems possessed.

Samantha works constantly, while in the Lazy Boy, where sleep overwhelmed her on the fateful night of Daniel's death. In her mind, his soul remains in the middle, trying to clean the mess seemingly left behind. There's a task to do in a hurry, and as Samantha reviews family videos, she must find bits and pieces of Daniel for a new video. This video must feature him happy, joking, as he did many, many, times. It's a difficult task but she's up to the challenge. Everyone thinks she's still in shock, while refusing to view his body or attend the funeral.

"She's in denial, still in shock," many of them say. "Just leave her alone to deal with it."

Samantha knows she's doing exactly what Daniel wants as she continues with the videos. There are at least thirty videotapes, six hours each, to edit. Daniel's soul remains to guide her through the process. Feeling fortunate to have bought a double VCR player/recorder right before his physical death, she hasn't yet learned there are no coincidences. The purchase made the plan work.

Family members note she needs the closure of seeing

Daniel's dead body. They demand that she eventually "faces reality" to admit he's gone.

Samantha sleeps in the chair for a number of days. As when physically alive, Daniel still telepathically communicates. Samantha hears him clearly. Although no audible words are spoken, his thoughts flow freely from the Otherside as she sits in the dark living room, with closed blinds. (11) She doesn't share this information knowing that everyone will call her crazy.

Rachel schedules Daniel's funeral for the day after the viewing at the church where they married. Samantha still feels driven to work on the videotape, even when Esther comes to console her from Michigan. A great, unexplainable urge to finish the video consumes her.

"You've been through enough Mom," Samantha hears Daniel say each time anyone asks her to attend the funeral. "You don't need to go to the dog and pony show."

Everyone looks at her as if she's crazy when she says Daniel does not want her at the funeral. (12)

Friends visit to offer condolences and deliver food before continuing on to the funeral. Rebecca's friend since high school, Lydia, her husband Joseph, and mother Hannah, arrive to set up tables in the back yard for the wake. Samantha hasn't met Joseph or Hannah who has brain cancer and wears a red bandana upon her shaved head. Their helpfulness soon overwhelms her.

The trio sets up chairs and tables, and puts food on kitchen counters, as Samantha continues to work. Later in the day, Hannah talks with Samantha of her recent move to Lydia and Joseph's house and ongoing cancer treatments. She writes a lovely poem for Abigail about Daddy Daniel in Heaven. Hannah ends the poem with "Amen." Lydia announces that all of Hannah's poems end the same special way.

Daniel's soul doesn't want sorrow but knows people have to deal with physical death. Few people attend the wake compared to those who attend the funeral. Some of Daniel's closest friends choose not to come. Samantha isn't sure why, but really doesn't care, as Daniel's soul directs her to distribute videotapes, for interested friends and family.

Samantha remains busy, making copies of the master videotape. The finished video makes it easy to see who Daniel really was. It covers his life from age seventeen to thirty-six years of age. There isn't much more to add since the family saw him increasingly less during his last year of life. She has not even considered visiting with Daniel's wife and daughter since the accident. When they arrive with the rest of their family, she's happy but feeling a bit guilty. Samantha finally leaves her task when people move out to the back yard.

A strong gust of air blows past as she opens the back screen door. Daniel's unmistakable presence flows joyously in the wind. He's happy to be free. The feeling is undeniable. Samantha's knees weaken and she nearly drops to the ground.

"I'm free Mom," Daniel shouts inside her brain. "I'm free!"

Her heart fills with joy even as tears flow down fat, red cheeks. But she doesn't tell anyone fearing that they'll think her crazy. It's the first of many times that she feels his presence so strongly. [13]

Daniel's Aunt Claudia arrives to surprise Samantha minutes later. Ruth telephoned her the day after Daniel died. Claudia and her husband had already planned to be in Florida, vacationing from Michigan, at the time of the funeral. Daniel had just reconnected with his father Peter's side of the family in 1997. Before then, he hadn't seen them for twenty-four years.

Samantha remembered the year Daniel said he wanted to find his father. He was angry, wondering why Peter never tried to find him. Daniel hoped to find a rich Peter to make up for all the years they missed. Samantha searched the Internet and found his address but when she telephoned, Peter wasn't there. She finally found a telephone number for his older Cousin Joe in Michigan. Daniel was then able to talk with Joe's mother, Aunt Claudia, letting her know he wanted to see his father.

Later that year Daniel, Samantha and Uncle Amos went to Michigan for Uncle Aaron's wedding. Daniel and Samantha also visited with the family he longed for. Daniel was thrilled to see his Aunt Claudia, Cousin Eunice, and Aunt Bathsheba. Cousin Joe wasn't there nor was Daniel's father. It quickly became obvious that Peter's family tree held just as many separations between family members as Samantha's did. No one knew where the "wanderer" was but learning of two stepbrothers and two more uncles made Daniel feel like winning a casino jackpot. Daniel remembered his stepbrother Scotty, born before Peter and Samantha divorced. He then learned that Peter, Bathsheba, and Anna were born when Daniel's grandmother Elisabeth married her third husband Beau. Peter had now left his second wife to travel, checking in with his family occasionally.

A surprised Rachel opened their front door seven months later to see Peter's wide grin. He spent several weeks in late June and early July getting to know his son. Daniel learned many things during that time. He also knew, without a doubt, that he was not going to get any money from Peter who remained unemployed most of the time. Peter lived with Daniel and Rachel for less than a month. After two weeks, Peter got a part time job working on computers at the public library. He left Daniel a computer, built using parts discarded by others. A very disgusted Daniel found child pornography stored on the computer.

Several family members listened to disappointed Daniel grieve about how Peter lived. Samantha was the first person he confided in.

"Mom, I'm sorry," he said. "For all these years I've

blamed you for taking me away from Peter. Now I see you did the right thing."

Samantha watched tears swell in Daniel's eyes and as they flowed down cheeks, she cried along with him.

Daniel never saw Peter again but continued to keep in touch with his Aunt Claudia through cards and telephone calls. He took Rachel to meet his Michigan family as well. And now, Claudia, like everyone else, is in a state of shock. She can't believe that after finally reconnecting with Daniel, he's dead.

"I got a hold of Peter to tell him about Daniel," Claudia notes. "He's living in Georgia but wasn't sure you'd want him to come so he stayed home. He has a little girl now."

"Daniel," Samantha replies, "was Peter's son too. He would have been welcome at the funeral and wake."

Samantha now feels guilt over taking Daniel away from his grandparents. Family secrets creep out of dark closets while explaining why she removed Daniel from their lives.

"I had to stop telling you where Daniel and I were," Samantha says holding back tears. "Peter started sniffing glue when I worked midnights. He couldn't keep a job and I had to support us. He started using heroin and kept stealing the money for our bills. When I wouldn't tell him where the money was, he beat us and tore the house apart until he found it. It was the only way I knew to protect us."

Telling Claudia the truth made Samantha feel better.

Claudia speaks as Samantha wipes at tears rolling down her face.

"I don't know if Peter ever told you Samantha but Beau wasn't the best of father's. He didn't treat Peter very well. He beat him with a razor strap and made him sleep in the basement."

Everything about their relationship now makes sense. Peter abused her and Daniel because he was abused. He merely repeated the cycle of abuse. Samantha, now feeling better, quickly leaves to keep her appointment with the dental specialist.

X-rays again fail to show anything abnormal. Fed up, Samantha tells the specialist to pull the tooth. She's not in the mood to get another root canal. A missing tooth doesn't seem so bad after losing Daniel. The specialist cuts through, and removes, a four-tooth bridge to pull the offending tooth.

An unforgettable relief overcomes Samantha as the specialist extracts her tooth. As she drives back to the house on 47th Drive, a nagging thought, about how women got their teeth pulled on purpose after losing a child in ancient times, preys on her mind.

The house on 47th Drive appears full of drunks when Samantha returns. Everyone talks about the last time they saw Daniel. Jeremiah, one of Daniels best friends and the last to see him alive, appears more upset than anyone else does.

Daniel went to his acupuncture treatment alone earlier in the day and then to visit his friend Tim. Tim decided it was time to go to bed after they had a few drinks. Daniel left his house and went up to the bar several blocks away. He telephoned Tim minutes later to ask if he would come up and have another drink with him. Tim told him he was already in bed. Daniel drank for two more hours.

Samantha shudders at the thought that the bar was less than six blocks away from where she sat in her living room.

Jeremiah now speaks in a hushed voice, afraid that no one will believe him.

"Daniel came to our house after he left the bar. He wanted a drink."

It was clear to both Jeremiah and his wife Judith that Daniel was drunk. After refusing to offer alcohol, they begged him for several minutes to sleep on the couch. Daniel said he had to get home because of plans with Rachel and Abigail. He hugged them both.

"Bro, you know that I love you," he told Jeremiah wrapping arms around him. "I love you guys," he repeated turning to walk out the door.

Jeremiah filled with indecision as Daniel's motorcycle cut through the silence of night like a sharp knife. By the time he rushed to the door to stop Daniel from leaving it was too late.

"I swear to God Daniel glowed white that night," Jeremiah now notes sheepishly. "I saw him as I stood by the front door and he was just white. I can't explain it. I started to go toward him but he drove away. As the motorcycle moved the white light just surrounded him."

Samantha senses Jeremiah speaks the truth and breaks into another round of sobs. (14)

Much to her dismay, several family members and friends now want to visit the accident site. She still fails to feel a desire to go and hears Daniel telling her to stay home. Esther stays behind to console her as the group piles into vehicles. The troop reports that they left flowers and gifts for him by the side of the highway upon returning hours later.

Many people appear to feel guilt over Daniel's passing, especially those consciously distanced from him. They missed important events in his life like his marriage to Rachel. Others, like Jeremiah and Judith, were with him on the day of his death. Samantha suspects that it's part of their contracts to learn and teach valuable lessons and to "wake-up" as she's doing. (15)

Some humans, maybe all humans, choose their own clues before birth to prompt them so they'll "wake-up" from this dream we call life. Samantha spent a lot of time before Daniel's birth trying to choose his name. His initials had to be a word and she finally decided on DAD. Daniel was very adamant about not having a child. It was a point of dispute for both of the women he loved.

Samantha felt lucky to have programmed in so many friends and family to help her deal with grief. One friend noted, "There's no way over-under-or around grief, you just have to slog through it, however long it takes. Be patient with it. You will heal in time." The words rang true as she thanked God and continued to heal.

    11. Ernest Holmes notes mental telepathy operates through Universal Mind. "It is only when the instrument is properly adjusted to some individual vibration that a clear message may be received."
    The receiver must tune in to the sender. Fortunately, most people receive only messages matching their own vibration.

    12. Silence remains Samantha's best ally even though she knows her connection with Daniel will never be broken. Even if he reincarnates, his soul will come when she needs him. Yet, her reliance on him will lessen as he leads her to souls on higher levels.

    Emmanuel notes, "The connection of love is never broken." Love's golden chain is eternal, always reaching out when there is genuine need, calling the soul wherever it may be.

    13. In The Afterlife Experiments, *it notes that electromagnetic energy within the body continues to circulate after death. This energy extends out into space and upon death is "freed" to "have all the consciousness, intent, and personality" of all that has occurred during physical life. There are people who view this occurrence as the soul and spirit now seeing with "new eyes."*

    14. Daniel will guide Samantha to Science of Mind teaching during the following year. Reading the major work of Ernest Holmes, she will know what happened to Daniel as he drove his motorcycle for the last time. A certain inner sense, Holmes notes, sees Reality at certain times in a flash that illuminates the whole being with a great flood of light. Mystics have seen this Cosmic Light and people have sensed that Truth is Light. *The Light came as Daniel's consciousness expanded.*

Nearly four years later, Samantha will read Spiritual Alchemy and learn that the soul's primary essence is pure white light. This vibrating energy source is the eternal connection to Universal Consciousness. Dr. Page tells us, "When the soul's consciousness is fully expressed, pure white light is seen, an event termed enlightenment." Samantha knew Daniel experienced that moment as Jeremiah watched.

15. A Course in Miracles *lets us know that in this illusionary world, sin represents the past, guilt represents the present, and fear represents the future. Most people at the wake drank themselves into oblivion not realizing they were dwelling on the past and the present. Living in the Now, knowing there is only one perfect state of love and forgiveness and that we live within that One, releases the need to feel any negativity. There is no sin, no guilt, and no fear in the Now.*

It's not easy to explain how there is no need for sin, guilt, or fear but A Course in Miracles *does it well. Ignoring the Truth, we make contracts with souls to interact with here on earth before we are born. We are born into human form after our souls design the details of our new mind-body life on earth. The tricky part of the process is that we agree to forget who we really are, spirits in human form, in a dream. We agree to forget that being human is just a game.*

Nothing in this or any universe is what it appears to be. Everything is just a projection of the mind. Humans remain unconscious of the true reality, as they appear to live in a world of duality. A "sick thought system," shared by everyone in this false universe, dominates the unconscious mind. God didn't create this world of duality, humans did. God knows only unconditional Love so it's not the nature of God to create anything of this world. Consciousness is the domain of the ego and humans, as souls, agree to not wake-

up until it is time to do so. We may, or may not, have fulfilled our so-called contracts when we begin to wake-up. And we may not wake-up until we leave our mind-body. Yet, we are all here to be teacher's of God. Some human beings come to that awareness sooner than others do.

There are so many clues for us to tap into when we're ready to: movies such as "Chances Are" and "The Matrix;" songs such as "Serenade" by the Steve Miller Band, "The Wall" by Kansas, and "Silent Lucidity" by Queensrÿche. There are numerous books, commercials, and even common sayings with the word "wake-up" that tell us things like, "Wake-up and smell the coffee." All of these are meant to prompt our little mind to wake-up to the fact that we are spirits in human form, part of One Mind.

In later years, Samantha will get many clues from books. One clue, while reading <u>Ultimate Journey</u>, will prompt her mind more than others will. Monroe notes, "The entry ramps to the Interstate is physical death as perceived by most human minds." The words will not surprise her as she remembers her son's choice to die on Interstate 95.

:-)

~ 7 ~
Big Changes Ahead

Guilt overcomes Samantha with thoughts of Daniel. It shocks her to remember joking about choosing a younger man to marry because widowhood would not be a part of life. There was already enough trauma and pain to deal with. Samantha now faces something much worse, realizing she agreed, as a soul, to lose her first-born. She now feels responsible for events leading to his death.

Things were never perfect for Rachel and Daniel. He came to Samantha for advice and support many times. Those times increased after Abigail's birth. Samantha knew things were not as they should be. It was hard to hold tears back when she learned of Daniel's hardships. Since it hurt to see Samantha cry over his troubles, Daniel began to confide in other family members.

Intuition is strong in Daniel's close-knit family. Rachel announced her pregnancy and the baby, they all sensed, would not be a big part of their lives. The limited times they saw pretty, brown-haired Abigail for months after her birth confirmed beliefs. Most of the women resigned themselves to not seeing her. Samantha knew it was only a matter of time before Abigail's treasured visits with her would stop. She filled her beloved granddaughter with love and family values hoping it would make a difference in years to come.

Joy was now much more prominent in Daniel and Rachel's life. She moved in with them before Abigail was a year old. Daniel began to look for places where he could be himself, without the fear of criticism. He stayed in his newly built workshop in the back yard as much as possible when home. Samantha's visits with Abigail began to lessen as Joy's role in their life increased. To her, it seemed as if

Abigail and Daniel were treated as possessions. Every gift Daniel's family gave to Abigail disappeared. Joy replaced it with something "better." Samantha grew tired of being silent as people taught Abigail how to shop, and collect possessions, instead of spend time with family. She couldn't figure out why this, and other odd things, happened but she knew something was very wrong.

Daniel's job promotion caused a ripple of change affecting everyone. Now he spent much more time away from home for the drive to work was more than an hour each way. Rachel found a house closer to his workplace when Abigail was 19-months-old. Daniel came to tell Samantha the news.

"I don't know what to do," he said. "The commute to work is killing me but I don't want to move away from the family and my friends. Yet, I think if we move Joy will find someplace else to live."

"You've got to do what is best for you, Rachel, and Abigail," she said hugging him tightly while feeling a familiar sense of loss in her gut.

The next Saturday, Daniel came alone to show her their new house before they signed the papers. It was important to him that Samantha approved of their country home. Daniel quickly drove to his new house using the Interstate. It took a little more than an hour to get there.

Stunned Samantha sat looking out at the large lot beyond an electronic gate. Daniel had to get out of his truck to open it. The house was beautiful and larger than any they lived in before with more than an acre of land. It looked perfect for them with a small pond and plenty of space in the house. Samantha knew she would see less of them but approved of the purchase. Daniel's family soon called it a palatial estate because it was much more than any of them ever dreamed of owning.

Joy remained close to Rachel after they moved to their dream home but she stayed behind and moved in with someone else. Samantha tried her best to be supportive and helpful as Daniel and Rachel adjusted to their new home and parenthood. They had spent all of Rachel's pregnancy swearing that Abigail's birth would not change how they lived. Now they were realizing that having Abigail made a huge difference in every part of life. They adored the blue-eyed, smart toddler who looked more like Daniel every day.

The days of washing dishes and tarring roofs for a living were far behind Daniel. He was the big boss man now. After twenty years, he finally had a career he loved and was happy to be close to his job. Rachel was elated to have a beautiful house in a great neighborhood. Everything seemed fine for a few months.

One day Samantha got an unexpected email addressed from Daniel. It said he knew she could not visit them as frequently as Joy did. The email confused her. She'd been waiting for an invitation to visit after announcing her intention to visit whenever they wanted her to. It was difficult to tell who sent the email as both Daniel and Rachel used the same email address. Samantha replied to the email letting them know she and James could visit them one weekend a month.

The family celebrated an unusual Christmas that year. They started a Florida tradition of bowling on Christmas Eve when on vacation there many years ago. Daniel and Rachel added a tradition of their own a few years after they met. At first, they saw their friends after the family bowl but in recent years, spent Christmas Eve with friends. The family missed seeing them at the annual bowl. This year, Daniel was sick with the flu. He called to let them know but no one was home so he left a message. It sounded to Samantha like it took great effort for Daniel to talk so she kept the recorded message on her computer with the others.

"Hey Mom, it's me. Are you home? Okay, see you in the morning. Love you. Say bye Abigail," he then said to his daughter. "Say bye, bye, Nana."

"Hi Nana," Abigail said.

Daniel's condition worsened on Christmas morning. When he threw up on the kitchen counter, he knew he was going to miss Christmas with his family to stay alone in bed. Rachel and Joy brought Abigail to see them but said they felt sick as well. The drive was tiring so they didn't stay long. Before leaving, Rachel invited everyone to the zoo to celebrate Abigail's second birthday the next day. Samantha decided not to go thinking they would delay the adventure until everyone was well.

Days later, Samantha took the Christmas tree down earlier than usual. She stripped the tree of scented pine needles before James carried it to the curb but had no idea why. A sense of unexplainable doom surrounded her while filling several, large containers with pine needles before storing them in a closet. Four years later, it became clear why she saved the scented needles from the Christmas tree. [16] She never hosted Christmas again in the house on 47th Drive.

Samantha now found it increasingly hard to travel for she took eight prescriptions and each one had certain "rules." Doctors prescribed more drugs to deal with medication side effects. Every additional drug seemed to decrease her quality of life. Drug toxicities were an increasing issue. Samantha added six supplements to try and lessen the effects of prescribed drugs. Research on P450 drug interactions resulted in a list of what to take and when. Samantha considered drug inhibitors, activators, and substrates. It paid off as side effects such as nausea and vomiting lessened but travel was still difficult.

Daniel's health was failing as well. His relationship with Rachel was quickly becoming more volatile. Joint and back pain required an increasing amount of prescription painkillers so he joined Rebecca, every two weeks, to visit an acupuncturist. Daniel missed his family. He wasn't used to seeing them so infrequently but there never seemed to be a good time to visit.

Samantha telephoned the couple in early February offering to watch Abigail so they could go out for dinner on Valentine's Day. She looked forward to spending quality time with Abigail. Medications, Samantha noted, dictated Papa and Nana's arrival time wherever they went.

Rachel soon emailed to say it would be wonderful for James and Samantha to come and stay the weekend. Abigail missed her nana and Papa very much.

Samantha was elated to hear Daniel's noisy truck in the driveway one morning before the scheduled visit. The computer in Daniel's Chevy truck needed repair and since the repair shop was near James and Samantha's house he decided to visit. Samantha ran to the den door, opened it, and stepped out to greet Daniel and Abigail joyfully. She asked if he got her email reply offering to visit once a month. Daniel's evasive answer led her to believe he had not seen the email. Samantha again made it clear that she would visit once a month, just like Joy did, with or without James. Daniel then left Abigail for a few hours while they worked on his truck. Samantha happily videotaped the visit.

When Daniel returned he didn't seem in a hurry to leave for he fell asleep on the couch. He talked with his mother about his life when he woke up. Daniel was resigned to living a life he didn't really enjoy. He wasn't happy at home but said he'd never leave his precious Abigail.

An invitation for Daniel's thirty-seventh birthday arrived days after he left with Abigail in his loving arms. Two-year-old Abigail wrote the invitation herself while Mommy Rachel helped with postage and mailing.

Valentine's Day weekend appeared to help build a more cohesive relationship for Daniel and Rachel. Rachel's six-year-old wedding ring mysteriously lost its diamond so Daniel replaced it. He also bought Abigail a beautiful gold chain necklace, which Samantha thought a bit too expensive for a two-year-old.

James and Samantha arrived at the house early

Saturday afternoon. Samantha hoped their visit would lessen the strain of her relationship with Rachel. Possessiveness filled the air when she was near Abigail so she stayed away from her granddaughter when Rachel was near. As usual, Samantha agreed with everything that Rachel said to avoid problems.

The thirty-hour visit appeared pleasurable for everyone. Abigail seemed happy to spend time with her papa and Nana while her parents ate at a local restaurant. James and Samantha enjoyed their meal of stuffed lobster that Daniel and Rachel bought for them. Before James and Samantha returned home the following evening, they promised to visit at least once a month.

Everyone celebrated Daniel's last birthday the following weekend. The events that took place set the scene for his death. The party was a gala event and just about every one of Daniel's friends came. Even the best friend, estranged from him for years, arrived to surprise him.

Neighbors from their old neighborhood, new friends, and co-workers arrive to see Daniel and Rachel's big, new house. It's such a beautiful day and the party has already begun when James, Samantha, and Samuel arrive. Samantha senses an uncomfortable hush in the air as they enter the house. Most of the women huddle around the kitchen. After a cursory greeting, Rachel sharply tells Samuel he cannot go into the bedroom to play the PlayStation games he and Daniel usually play.

Samuel disappointed and upset, at the prospect of not being able to lull his over-active mind with games, sulks. Rebecca is delayed so he's ridden with James and Samantha hoping to keep busy. Thinking it best to avoid a scene, Samantha takes him outside to sit at the table on the back screened in porch. Except for a few people in the back yard, everyone else remains in the house. It now becomes a chore for Samantha to keep Samuel entertained.

Samuel runs off to play in the yard within an hour but

Samantha decides to sit at the table by herself. Feeling uncomfortable, she now watches the other women sample several alcoholic creations through the sliding glass door. She's not bothered to be alone for it's worth the cost of not having the usual expected trauma.

It feels good to be outside in the middle of winter where the wind blows softly and the air temperature is just right. The smell of sweet, country air fills Samantha's nostrils. As she focuses between Samuel and other boys in the yard, and people inside the house, Rachel's friend Reba comes out to sit at the bar in front of her. She's been with the other women in the kitchen making frozen blender drinks. Samantha looks toward her to speak.

"It's such a beautiful day. It is the perfect day to be outside."

Rachel quickly struts out onto the porch to stand next to Reba's bar stool. Samantha goes into "alert mode" sensing something is about to happen. With a flip of her head toward Rachel, Reba asks, "How many people do you expect?"

Rachel silently glares at Samantha.

"Well," Samantha notes apologetically, Rebecca's running a little late but should be here with Mom and Terrance in about an hour. Daniel asked her for a special gift so she's at the store now."

Samantha doesn't tell them the gift is a number of crystals to help Daniel heal his ills.

"I would think she'd have gotten his present before the day of his party," Rachel answers angrily.

Samantha quietly replies.

"She's going to a special store that's not open at night and she works during the day so she can't go then."

"I know what she's getting him," Rachel notes sharply, raising her voice. "I work too but I could have gotten it before today."

"Well, she did just start a new job so it's difficult for her to take time off right now."

Rachel's glare looks ugly and Samantha realizes she is going to have another one of her "fits." She tries to remember what to do. Last time, it happened when Samantha watched both Abigail and Samuel. The fight with Samuel started when Rachel arrived after work to get Abigail. She hadn't known he'd be there. Samantha told Samuel to run into the bedroom and lock the door but that hadn't worked out well at all. Rachel banged on the door demanding that 11-year-old Samuel open it to apologize. It was hard for Samantha to deal with as she heard him crying on the other side of the door.

Samantha now thought hard. What was it Daniel told her to do after the episode in Fort Myers? Would the discussion between Rachel and Samantha have escalated to a fistfight if Daniel hadn't stepped out into the hall to get between them? Had Daniel told her to walk away or agree with Rachel? Samantha couldn't remember so she tried to look calm.

Rachel's voice rose as she continued.

"I am so f**king tired of hearing about how Rebecca works and I don't. I work just as much as she does. I am so f**king tired of hearing about how great Rebecca is and how much she does."

"I didn't say that Rachel."

"But you implied it."

Rachel continues to go on, and on, about how she's always victimized by Daniel's family. It's clear to Samantha that Rachel is jealous of Daniel's love for his younger sister.

"And I am outraged that she borrowed $2,000 from Daniel," Rachel yells. "That's my money too and I want it back."

"You weren't supposed to know about that," pops right out of Samantha's mouth.

She sits in shock as Daniel comes out of the house to sit quietly behind the bar, looking out at the three women. Samantha wonders if Daniel knows what's happening. She thinks about the thousands of dollars given to Daniel when he was out of work, the $2,000 given to both he and Rebecca when she finally got a child support check a few years before. Samantha considers the thousand or so that Rebecca loaned Daniel and Rachel when they needed it. And she dwells on the diamond and the gold necklace Daniel just bought.

Daniel sits quietly while Rachel rants on as a woman possessed with hate. Horrified Samantha sits like a stone, thinking about how Rebecca struggles to get back on her feet, after major surgery and eight-months of disability. Rebecca just left her abusive boyfriend after eight years and is finally able to start a new, less strenuous career. The last thing she needs is more abuse. Although Samantha is appalled and outraged, she once again apologizes.

"I'm sorry if I said something that upset you Rachel. I didn't mean to imply that you didn't work."

Samantha feels her face and neck flushing and wonders if she brought along extra blood pressure medicine. She continues to apologize as Rachel continues to speak badly of her and Rebecca. And then she realizes, this isn't about Rachel and herself at all. It's something else. And no matter what she does, or says, Rachel will continue to rant and yell until she's sure that Samantha is sufficiently embarrassed and humiliated. Samantha sits there and lets her continue, hoping it will be over soon.

It saddens her that Daniel says only, "I wish that you all could respect the fact that this is my birthday and get along."

With that, he gets up and leaves the porch to reenter the house.

Rachel looks at Samantha with a smirk as soon as the door closes behind him. She stops yelling and stomps into the house with Reba following her. Samantha is left alone feeling victimized once again. Rachel, she believes, is one of those people in the *Nasty People* book needing to invalidate others to boost their own self-esteem.

Rebecca enters the porch with her grandmother, Terrance, and his teenage son Joel minutes later. Samantha briefly tells Rebecca what happened so she reenters the house to make sure Samuel stays safe. By now, they all know Rachel's method of operation but they don't know their souls agreed to try and learn lessons from her.

There's a time and purpose for everything but Samantha doesn't know this yet. She turns toward the side window to see Abigail, staring out at her, clutching a new dolly. Abigail's knees are close to her chest as she hides behind the curtain. Samantha quickly takes Abigail's picture and then notices the crocodile tears. Abigail looks severely distressed.

Tears stream down Abigail's little, heart-shaped face as she looks at Samantha. Her frown tears at Samantha's heart. Not knowing what Abigail saw, she slowly rises to slip quietly into the house. She sits down next to Abigail and pulls the sheer white curtain around them. And then she gently pulls Abigail up onto her lap to ask her what is wrong.

Tears continue to trickle from Abigail's beautiful, blue eyes. They run down her face as Samantha strokes her hair while telling her it will be okay. Daddy will make it all right. Samantha doesn't know where the words come from. Rachel and Joy stand yards away in the kitchen talking about making more blender drinks with Reba and Rachel's best friend Patti. Samantha hopes they don't see her holding Abigail for it's always a struggle to hold her when Rachel and Joy are near.

Abigail stops crying and rests her head in Samantha's lap as she continues to stroke her long, brown hair. She feels hot so Samantha asks if she wants a drink of milk or juice. After Abigail answers juice, Samantha slowly puts her down and walks into the kitchen. She knows if she makes a big deal of Abigail's crying Rachel or Joy will take her away and she'll lose her chance to hold her a bit. Rachel looks at

Samantha, acts as if nothing happened between them, and calmly speaks.
"What do you need."
"Abigail feels a bit hot so I thought I'd get her juice."
"She's had that flu or a cold for a while," Rachel replies. "My mom must have rinsed out her cup but you can get another one from the cupboard."
Samantha slowly gets the cup, fills it with juice, and returns to give it to Abigail. Joy walks over and quickly scoops Abigail up saying she has to change her.
Most of Daniel's family remains outside at the back porch table for the next few hours. Rachel and the other women stay in the kitchen mixing, and drinking, frozen alcoholic drinks. Samuel tries to stay clear of Rachel since her attack on him remains fresh in his memory. Rebecca occasionally gets him to go outside and play in the yard with Abigail, Daniel's friend Jude, and Reba's son, who is close to Samuel's age.
Terrance stays inside to keep a watchful eye on him when Samuel returns to the house. After a short while, a very angry Terrance ventures onto the porch to report that Rachel and Joy are talking about Samuel and Rebecca. Samuel is in the room next to them so he hears their conversation. They verbally attacked Terrance when he asked them to stop talking about Samuel and Rebecca.
The party finale occurs after Samantha carries out Daniel's store-bought cake. She usually makes Daniel a homemade birthday cake. This one is very large, rather heavy, and difficult to hold. By the time he blows out the candles, Daniel is helping Samantha hold the cake up for it's breaking in half.
Daniel's family now naively looks forward to playing their usual pinochle card game for he missed the last few games. His absence at Christmas is still fresh on their minds so they all look forward to spending the night. Guests are beginning to leave as Rebecca sits at the back porch table

shuffling cards.

The sweet smell of fresh, country air wafts around them as Samantha enjoys looking at trees common to native Florida. She periodically glances through sheer white curtains to see Samuel, curled up alone in the corner of the couch, playing his Gameboy. Abigail and Reba's son chase each other around the couch. As Samantha stares, Joy moves into the room to start talking to Samuel. She jabs her finger toward his face, several times, while speaking.

"You better go in and assess the situation," Samantha tells Rebecca with a nod toward them.

Rebecca quickly tosses cards aside and runs into the house. She calmly asks Joy to stop telling Samuel what to do. Joy viciously announces that Rebecca is a rotten mother and has not spent enough time with her child as a baby. That's why he has attention-deficit hyperactivity disorder (ADHD), a so-called bogus diagnosis.

It gets increasingly uncomfortable as the violence escalates. Samuel grows visibly upset as Joy continues her verbal, savage attack on Rebecca. Samantha remains on the back porch. Although she wants to help her daughter, she has had her share of humiliation for the day. Rebecca tearfully tells Samantha within minutes that she's leaving with Samuel.

Samantha knows it isn't good for kids to see such inappropriate behavior. She remembers a poem placed on the wall of Daniel's room when he was an infant. Words to "Children Learn What They Live" sticks in her mind. She can't remember who wrote it but she remembers one line of the poem. "If children live with criticism, they learn to condemn." She tells Rebecca that she and James will leave the party as well.

James, Daniel, and Reba's husband sit smoking cigars out on the back porch. Having no idea of what's occurred, they look settled in for the night as Samantha walks back outside to tell James they're leaving. He smiles and calmly asks to finish his cigar. She asks for the keys and says she'll wait for him in the van.

"What's wrong?" Rachel's friends ask as Samantha heads for the door.

"It's one thing for Rachel and Joy to verbally attack adults, but totally inexcusable to attack Samuel," she states moving quickly outside.

They look at one another in shock.

Years later, Samantha will truly understand what happened at, and before, the party. [17]

Samantha now hates the thought of her upset daughter driving. She moves through the two-car garage to hug her, knowing Rebecca and Samuel are going through a difficult transition period, living alone together for the first time. They're opening wounds to the psychologist who helps them deal with Samuel's ADHD. Her own effort with psychologists, and research of ADHD, leads Samantha to believe the day is more traumatic for them than others.

James walks outside within minutes choosing to leave his cigar behind. Samuel then climbs into the plush back seat of his sports van with Samantha while Grandma, Terrance, and Joel pile into Rebecca's little car. Joy ventures out to the front of the house as they back out of the drive. She looks at them while shaking her head as if she has no idea what happened. No one knows the events of the day are necessary for the souls' plan to work. Joy played her difficult but vital role very well.

Samuel bursts into tears as the van moves out of the driveway.

"Was the fight my fault? He asks as tears freely flow

down his round face. "Am I crazy?"

James and Samantha spend twenty minutes calming him down by assuring; he did nothing wrong. Samantha now resolves to end the humiliation of Daniel's family, at least in front of the children.

Much later, she reviews photos taken during Daniel's party to see many orbs all around him. It comforts her to know his spirit friends never left him alone and indeed guided the day's events to ensure that all went according to the souls' plan.

16. The pinecone energetically stimulates the pineal gland. As Dr. Page notes, the essence of pine "is commonly used by those who wish to enhance their creative union between spirit and matter." The pineal gland is the prime center for controlling all of the body's endocrines. In <u>Life and Teaching of the Masters of the Far East</u> Baird T. Spalding notes, "It is the Master, the I AM of the physical body." The gland normally shrinks as we age. This atrophy divorces us from the Kingdom of Heaven.

17. Samantha's experience helps her to move forward in awareness of God. It's all part of a plan agreed to by everyone involved before human birth. Information concerning power games seems vital but Samantha doesn't know why. She, and other family members, are players and victims of power games, i.e. physic or energy field theft. Later while reading <u>Celestine Prophecy</u>, Samantha notes that someone highlighted information about energy stealing. She learns that Rebecca read the book before her.

Energy theft can lessen a person's confidence for humans are often fearful when threatened verbally or physically. They feel forced to pay attention to the person threatening them. This gives the "thief" their energy and helps them to feel stronger while the "victim" feels weaker.

People usually participate in power games and control others with words or actions on an unconscious level.

But they know that saying and doing certain things to other people makes them feel stronger. This damaging type of control over others sucks vital energy out of those dominated.

Socially isolated people, with low self-esteem and feelings of inadequacy, often play energy stealing games. Thieves have either forgotten how to create their own energy or have lost their spiritual connection to God, the Source. The theft is mainly linked to the lower three chakras and Dr. Page notes, it "creates a greater karma than any physical crime." It "mirrors the action of burglary, sexual abuse and the acquisition of land that is already inhabited by others."

Children and those who have a similar naïve view of life are easy victims. People at the highest risk of energy field theft include those with a need to be liked or needed. They may desire harmony at any cost and have a passion to help, or change others, as Daniel did. Some people may need approval or acknowledgment. Of special note, now much more related to current earth time, fearful people are at high risk of being the victims of power games.

We realize the Sixth Insight by recognizing how we steal energy from other people. Through awareness of this Insight Redfield notes, "our connection becomes more constant and we can discover our own growth path in life, and our spiritual mission – the personal way we can contribute to the world."

Being conscious of our control drama helps us to focus more clearly on our own path. Learning our own drama (intimidation, interrogation, aloofness, or poor me) frees us to become conscious of our actions. If we are aware, we can find a higher meaning for our lives. We can determine the spiritual reason we were born to our particular families.

The information sounded familiar but Samantha's understanding of energy stealing was far from complete. A habit she developed in childhood to get attention, Samantha learned, guided the way she stole other people's energy. Yet, one could obtain energy without stealing it from others. Samantha had no idea how important this information would be to her life's purpose for she unknowingly chose to break that particular energy pattern within her soul group.

Samantha learns the key to stopping the game in later years. It's easier for people to give up their way of manipulating for energy if they feel energy coming in. Redfield notes how important it is to consciously send energy while looking beyond the drama at the real person (spirit) in front of you. And as Samantha's awareness grows, she knows that power games, just like everything else on earth, are illusions in a dream world. This thought helps her to get through the years.

According to Emmanuel, the soul's greatest need is self-love, which leads us to grow and dispels judgments. Self-love helps to unify for we are unable to accept others until we accept ourselves. Expansion comes through the heart and every bit of kindness, and love, which we give to others, adds more Light and power to God's Truth.

As Van Praagh notes in his book <u>Talking to Heaven</u>, "Ultimately we all are here to learn love. Without love and awareness of self, we will not know how to love others." Mastering the unconditional love of self, and others, helps us to become enlightened and respect the natural law of cause and effect because we know **it is the only way**.

<u>A Course in Miracles</u> helps us to understand more about the illusory dream world of power games. Perception, a form of energy, didn't exist until we, as individualized parts of God, decided to dream about separation from God. Separation includes all kinds of levels, degrees, aspects, and intervals. Energy, Renard rightly notes, is in the domain of perception. It is not true reality because it changes. God does not change, period.

:-)

~ 8 ~
Time to Wake Up

Samantha puts party pictures on her desktop computer the next day. She enlarges and prints the one of Abigail crying; she must be sure it looks as bad as remembered. The frown and crocodile tears covering Abigail's red cheeks are hard to ignore. Sadness and anger consume her.

Verbal attacks occur when Daniel's family tries to interact with Abigail, in the presence of Rachel or Joy. Not wanting to see Abigail cry, Samantha decides she will never subject herself to hostility again. Samantha resolves to end the abuse by not seeing Abigail in their presence. She hopes this decision will also spare Abigail, and Samuel, from unnecessary trauma. Samantha tapes the picture to her computer desk as a reminder.

She looks at the picture and waits in vain to get an apology from either Rachel or Daniel. The thought of Abigail seeing, hearing, or being the focus of verbal attacks tears at her heart. After two weeks, she decides to alert Abigail's parents to the unhealthy habit by emailing a short note, along with the picture of her crying.

"Maybe," Samantha thinks, "the email will open their minds to realize what's going on." That will make her effort worthwhile. They will be angry after reading it but she just doesn't care, for this is her battle. Samantha has to make them see that what Abigail sees, and hears, as a child will mold future actions. She made many mistakes raising Daniel and Rebecca and now wants to spare her grandchildren from abuse.

"Wake UP," Samantha writes in the emails subject line. "Here's a picture of Abigail after she watched her mother's irrational, hostile and caustic outburst on me for NOTHING that was my fault at your birthday party Daniel.

This attack was only one of many since I've met Rachel. The attack was followed by an attack on Terrance, and then Samuel and Rebecca by Joy.

"I will no longer put Abigail in situations where she is subjected to this kind of behavior. Do not expect me to visit your home until these kinds of attacks are stopped. Rachel and Joy went way TOO FAR this time."

Samantha sends the note quickly without thinking.

Since they missed their pinochle card game at Daniel's party, the family meets at Terrance's house on Sunday. Still upset, they want to discuss the party. The rest of the family knows of Samantha's email. She asks everyone to read it and see the picture of Abigail before the game begins.

"My blood pressure is still high," she announces, with a sigh, while they pass the paper, "after taking double my medication. If you continue to discuss this, I'll leave."

They quietly drop the subject.

Rachel answers Samantha's email days later. It seems she saw things differently.

"Maybe a little more thought should have gone into your insulting me in front of my friend and my husband," Samantha reads with great distress. Rachel continues to note that Samantha is not around enough to see how hard she works to make a better life for Daniel and Abigail. "As for Joy," Rachel announces, "I have no jurisdiction over her and her actions. She is an adult and can make any kind of comment she prefers."

Rachel's well-described feelings now confuse Samantha. Did Samantha really display dislike for Rachel and her family over the years? Did she and her family continuously brow beat Rachel?

"Unfortunately for you," Rachel continues, "I'm going to be around for a long time. I love my husband and daughter very much and am sorry you feel this way about me. Hopefully, someday things will change and you can stop trying to change me into someone else."

"Abigail is a wonderful little girl and I am sorry if you do not put your own selfish feelings aside for her sake, as I have many, many times. I hope you can understand things from a mother's point of view," Rachel notes before ending the communication.

A very angry Daniel telephones the next day. It's the worse telephone call Samantha ever receives as he relays how she disrespected his wife at his birthday party. Her body reacts violently, shaking while listening to Daniel talk. It appears that her actions caused the loss of a beloved son. As she listens, Samantha hears all of Rachel's words, coming through Daniel's mouth.

"You have never accepted Rachel and Joy as family," he shouts.

Samantha recalls many years of Christmas celebrations with Rachel, Joy, her ex-husband and son. She remembers cooking the Christmas turkey, wrapping their presents, and stuffing Christmas stockings so they wouldn't feel left out.

"You have always put Rachel and Joy down and never had a kind word to say about them," Daniel yells.

Samantha recalls how everyone in Daniel's family heard Joy and Rachel gossip about them. She remembers how, because of Joy's hostility, Daniel's side of the family didn't come for Christmas dinner in 2002. Most of them enjoyed Christmas dinner at Ruth and Naomi's house that year, choosing to come only for dessert. Samantha listened to Joy then as she laughed and repeatedly noted how nice it was to have quiet, without "those negative complaining lesbians." Samantha felt bad thinking she betrayed Ruth and Naomi when she failed to disagree with Joy. Yet, she kept her mouth shut to avoid Christmas Day conflicts.

Now as Daniel yells over the phone, Samantha realizes what he says happened on the porch is not at all how it occurred in her memory. Daniel seems unaware of what Rachel said to her. The way he recounts the "party episode" matches Rachel's way of thinking. Rachel turns the tide by convincing Daniel that his mother humiliated her. In Samantha's mind, a veil of ignorance covers him entirely now. He isn't acting in his usual sensitive and caring manner as a peacemaker. Samantha barely says a word as he yells and forbids her to send them email again. She feels ready to vomit as tears cascade, like a river, to pool on the floor.

Daniel hangs up on Samantha, for the first time, as his voice begins to hoarsen. Samantha falls to the floor crying over his loss, while clutching her legs in the fetal position. Daniel then phones his sister in tears. Rebecca calls Samantha quickly to verify that Daniel knows what he's said is untrue. He's sorry for yelling at his mother and is now distraught over the whole situation.

Samantha recalls the last time she felt the loss of Daniel. Rachel handed her a single, red rose during their wedding ceremony, and when she took it, shivers ran up her spine. No one knew she cried because she felt Daniel was lost to her. Yet, the feeling in her gut was undeniable at the time. Now she also cries for the loss of Abigail, even knowing Daniel did not mean what he said. He only acted as protector of his family, as she told him to do months before. He acted according to "the script."

Samantha feels driven to deal with the issue, while unsure of its characteristics, because she suspects it's an issue in other lives. She needs to "make things right" this time. She decides to write a letter to reinforce her decision to stop Rachel and Joy's abusive behavior. The letter isn't addressed to anyone but written quickly as words fill her head. The pen seems to move quickly by itself.

"Through the years, after becoming educated and getting counseling, I have tried to teach my children that hostile, caustic, and aggressive confrontation is inappropriate. It is even more inappropriate when practiced regularly by someone who uses this method of invalidation on people by whom they feel threatened.

"In my humble opinion, allowing this kind of behavior to continue, from a key role model in front of a child, only reinforces the belief that it is okay to belittle people in front of others and project ones inadequacies onto others. Until the core issues are dealt with, the behavior will most likely continue. Life skills counseling may be appropriate. People who tend to gossip about and judge others do so to avoid facing their own life issues. Many use projection, meaning they accuse others of what they do themselves.

"These hostile and inappropriate verbal attacks are not new to me. For the sake of family, I have put up with these attacks since before the wedding, at the wedding itself, and over the past seven years. I have been with Abigail when her mother verbally attacked Daniel, Samuel, Rebecca, and me on several occasions for no valid reason.

"I have heard her call Daniel names, such as bastard, in front of Abigail and tell her that "Daddy is leaving us," both of which are inexcusable. The first time Rachel verbally attacked me was in a public restaurant, when I barely knew her. She scolded me because Rebecca could not meet Rachel's scheduled bridesmaid dressing appointment due to her full time day job, night school, and caring for her son as a single mother.

"At the wedding itself, two major attacks on me personally and Daniel's entire family occurred that were totally inexcusable. As my father lay dying in a hospital bed, I had to be subjected once again to a public attack against me by Rachel in the hall of a hotel. The time Rachel ran through my home screaming at Samuel to apologize, with Abigail crying in her arms, and Samuel crying behind the closed bedroom door for something he had not done, was horrifying.

"I have watched everyone try their best to keep Rachel calm by building up her self esteem with praise, overlooking valid issues, and basically trying to be on guard so as to not 'set her off' or give Joy fuel to harm us. And I have 'sucked it up' every time Rachel has disrespected us all and tried to keep peace in the family; but now I see that this only leaves the path wider for Rachel and Joy to take advantage of our gracious behavior.

"This abuse must stop. I will no longer be involved in teaching Abigail, and Samuel, that hostile verbal attacks on people, especially for no reason, are normal or appropriate. I love Abigail and Samuel and I realize that their future actions as adults will be based on the actions of key role models.

"I feel very saddened knowing that Abigail has never really been allowed to visit with her father's family without some kind of confrontation. This behavior has happened even when we have been especially careful through our words and actions to not do anything that might be misconstrued. It has always been stressful and a chore to defend oneself against unwarranted verbal, and as happened to Rebecca, physical attacks as Rachel chased her down the street in front of Rebecca's friends.

"Now, when the attacks occur, despite careful monitoring of our behaviors and words, it is inexcusable to continue to allow oneself to be subjected to such abuse as that displayed by Rachel and Joy to myself, then Terrance, Samuel, and Rebecca on the occasion of my son's thirty-seventh birthday. I realize that they both may have had a bit too much alcohol to drink but that is no excuse.

"I live with enough stress daily, due to numerous medical conditions, without having to increase it by worrying about how my grandchildren will be affected by these verbal attacks and trying to 'tiptoe' around Rachel and Joy to avoid them. It is time to no longer be abused verbally for the sake of temporary family cohesiveness.

"I think that the best I can do, in order to be a good role model and protect my grandchildren, is to not put them in situations where they may be harmed again. I will do this by not having contact with Rachel or Joy as this is when the verbal attacks and hostile attitudes occur. I will try my best not to allow the children to be placed in a position where they are set up to experience more behavior that is inappropriate.

"I will no longer see Abigail in the presence of her mother, or Joy, and perhaps that action will spare Abigail from having to see this kind of inappropriate behavior again. As much as I am able, I will protect Samuel from this abuse as well. If Rachel and Joy seek the counseling that they appear to need, perhaps I'll change my mind when the threat is no longer there."

It felt good to write down what happened, to get it all out. Samantha wasn't quite sure what to do with her letter but as she printed and read it, she knew she'd give it to Daniel. Four years later, she will realize the full extent of her actions and purpose. [18]

18. Samantha is finally on her soul's chosen path. She is no longer willing to play the family's power games but it will be years before she learns exactly what to do. It's time to clear old patterns of suppression and raise consciousness to new levels of compassion and tolerance, without stealing energy.

Samantha's soul knows Abigail's self-worth suffers every time shame and abuse affects her.

As Dr. Page notes, bullying is common in homes where those bullied regain their self-esteem by shaming others "who are weaker and less able to answer back, such as children, partners and animals."

Human energy," Dr. Page stresses, "is more highly valued spiritually than any material or mineral wealth. In other words, one of the cost-effective forms of fuel is human power, especially from those who are young or in the flow of creativity. Energy stealing is happening all the time and is more successful when an individual is shamed, fearful or in despair, for then they will easily surrender their energy to the lowest bidder."

One person gains at the cost of another "and the cost to the weaker of the two may be their life as the more delicate systems of immunity, hematology, endocrinology and neurology take the brunt of the power loss."

This human drama, Samantha realizes, fatally affected Daniel. Increasing humiliation stripped him of self-respect and self-worth and robbed him of his power. Yet, Samantha knows Daniel agreed to live through the drama before he came into human form. Rebecca's words only weeks before his accident ring through her head.

"You know Mom; he's not as strong as we are."

Upon reading <u>Celestine Prophecy</u>, Samantha learns of the Seventh Insight and knows her personal mission. The flow of so-called coincidences guides her toward her destiny. The Seventh Insight becomes more real as answers arrive through dreams and intuitions. Eventually, she realizes, we are truly each other's angels as we synchronistically provide words of wisdom for one another. Samantha learns to stop judging others and start listening to the spirit within. And as Renard notes, since this is a dream world, it's not valid to judge anything. Yet on earth we can, "Judge ideas, not people. Then accept the true ideas."

:-)

~ 9 ~
The Last Visit

Countless thoughts of separation always filled Samantha's mind before Daniel's transition. Sensing many past lives and lifestyle changes in the current life, she knew it was again time to transition, even as the past continued to disturb. Detachment ruled. Someone else moved through the experiences but Samantha kept the memory of lessons learned. "Yeah," this someone thought. "God, what a life this one has been. I need to write a book."

Samantha wanted to help her family grow and contribute to the world. She believed that writing a book would help women who felt locked into abusive lifestyles. Surely, it would help them to realize they can change their own lives and leave the world a better place. Yet, it was difficult to get anything done because she wanted to enjoy the little things in life again, like the sun on her skin and the clouds as they rolled by in the sky.

Exhausted from doctors, tests, and treatments, Samantha was tired of getting back to a point where her quality of life was up to an eight, on the doctor's scale of ten, only to get another diagnosis with suggestions for more tests, invasive treatments, and surgeries that again decreased quality of life.

Restrictions ruled her world. Samantha was tired of not being able to eat and drink certain things, weary of taking medications, and worn-out fighting the nausea they caused. It bothered her when she had to drink more, and more, water just to get pills down past the lump in her throat. Because she wanted to stop hurting, to stop the constant pain in her body most of all, she continued to take the drugs hoping they would eventually help.

Samantha was tired of "sucking it up" when dealing

with inadequate people whose low self-esteem led them to try and make others feel bad. It was becoming more difficult to agree for the sake of keeping peace in the family, holding back thoughts derived out of more than fifty years of experience. Watching other people, and knowing their harmful words hurt Abigail and Samuel, exhausted her. She was tired of living life, as she knew it. There had to be a better way to live and she was going to find it.

Thoughts about her rarely seen granddaughter constantly haunted her. She began to do things differently, attending more family events instead of working on a failing business. Forcing herself out of the house, to watch Samuel play T-ball at the ball field, seemed to increase energy. The weather was hotter than she cared for but it felt good to breathe fresh air.

Although sweat rolled down her face, and the sun burned, it still seemed worth the effort to get out of the house. It made her feel more alive and part of the world again. She felt good while playing catch with the smaller kids even if the girls reminded her of Abigail. Samantha looked into one girls huge, brown eyes and tried to pretend they were blue like Abigail's, like Sherman's. She missed Abigail and Daniel terribly.

The "party episode" ran repeatedly in her brain. She wondered what could have prevented it, even while believing Rachel's verbal attack was part of their souls' contract. Samantha thought a change in her tone of voice, when replying to Rachel, might have made a difference. But she was tired of coddling her so she could see her son and granddaughter.

Daniel surprised Samantha with a telephone call nearly a month after his birthday party. He asked if she would watch Abigail the next day while he went to see the acupuncturist with Rebecca. A happy Samantha readily agreed. She was ecstatic to learn of his plan to go with his sister, at least once a month, leaving Abigail with Samantha during that time. She hung up the phone planning to videotape Abigail's visit for her extensive collection of family tapes.

Daniel was unaware of her plan to video their visit as she set up the camera in the corner of the living room. Samantha didn't know it would be the last video of her son as she set up the little table and chair, stored away, before they arrived the next day. She had taken the reminder of Daniel and Abigail apart, after Daniel's call, and hid it in the hall closet. She also placed all the toys back where Abigail last left them or could easily see them.

The video camera recorded the sound of Daniel's noisy SUV as it pulled into the drive. Abigail's loud crying filled the air as he opened the truck's door. For the first time, Daniel did not walk through the dining room to the living room where the video camera was set up. He carried her through the kitchen and into the hall that led to the living room.

They stood together in the small hallway as Abigail cried in his arms. Daniel apologized for yelling at Samantha through the telephone.

"I understand," Samantha said. But she wasn't quite sure that she did. She didn't say it was okay.

Daniel returned his attention to Abigail who appeared upset over being at Nana and Papa's house. She wanted to go back to Grandma Joy's house. They all spent a few minutes in the bathroom as Abigail proved what a big girl she was by going to the bathroom, all by herself.

Abigail calmed down and stopped crying after Samantha spoke softly to her but seemed very shy. Daniel kissed his beautiful daughter and told her he would return after his appointment. He lovingly handed her to Samantha who counted on two hours of caring for her. Abigail seemed more at ease as Samantha pointed out her toys and they began to play with them.

They had five precious hours together before Daniel

returned. Samantha knew he wanted her to have as much time with Abigail as possible. He didn't explain why it had taken him so long, and again avoided being filmed, even as he joined them on the floor to draw smiley faces.

As Daniel rose to leave, Samantha handed him copies of the four sheets of paper written weeks before. They held her account of what happened at his birthday party along with the page written twelve days before, while waiting for an apology. She told Daniel it would mean a lot if he read them. He glanced at the papers, shoved them in his back jeans pocket, and told her he would. Daniel then picked up Abigail while Samantha got her bag of toys. They joked and laughed all the way to his SUV.

Daniel put Abigail gently into her car seat, kissed and hugged Samantha and announced that he would see her later. After she again said goodbye and headed for the house, Daniel called her back. He stood in front of his SUV and paused, as if deciding what to say.

"Rachel and I will probably not be able to join you this year in the Keys," he noted looking down at the concrete drive.

Samantha said she understood and they kissed one another and hugged tightly again. Family vacation was different for the last two years so Samantha didn't seem surprised. Daniel and Rachel drove down to the Keys in their huge recreational vehicle (RV). The RV held both of their Skidoo's along with everything else needed. It was too big to go under the bridge to camp near the cabins where the rest of the family stayed. Daniel and Rachel camped at a spot almost two blocks away from the cabins. The entire family was disappointed to have Daniel further away. They all missed their usual closeness at mealtimes and card games. Daniel and Rachel also spent less time with them than in previous years. Daniel's mood, at the time, seemed to be less upbeat and the family worried about him.

Now as Samantha and Daniel stood in the driveway

in front of his SUV they seemed reluctant to let go of each other. Samantha finally began to walk towards the house again. Daniel called her back as he opened the driver's side door to his SUV.

"I'll bring Abigail by to visit with you at least once a month when I go with Rebecca to see the acupuncturist," Daniel noted before reaching out.

For the third time, they hugged tightly and kissed each other goodbye before he and Abigail drove away.

It was the last time she saw her son, the precious baby she planned to conceive at 15-years-old.

Watching the day's video, Samantha heard Daniel's voice but never saw the full image of his body. She found it very strange for Daniel always liked to be videotaped and made home movies fun by joking around in them but this time he avoided the camera. Samantha didn't think he knew the video camera was on. Clearly, his mind was distracted.

Rebecca asked for help days after Daniel's visit. In a constant state of panic, she suffered many ruptured, ovarian cysts over the past year. Now unemployed without health insurance, money was hard to get so going to the hospital emergency room was out of the question. Rebecca counted on being with Samantha when the pain got intense. She was always afraid of dying during the attacks. Rebecca took the pain pills prescribed by her doctor and together they waited for the cysts to rupture so the pain would stop. Samantha kept busy caring for Rebecca and forgot about everything else.

It seemed that Daniel, Rebecca, and Samuel were suffering just as much as Samantha was now. [19] Eleven-year-old Samuel stayed with his aunts because Rebecca did not want him to see her in pain. Samuel was doing better than before but was now on three medications. The doctors prescribed a drug for asthma, one for ADHD, and one for depression.

Enjoying robust health, James decided to take a week off to fish in the Everglades during the last few days of

March. He planned to return late on Sunday, April 4, 2004 but returned unexpectedly on Saturday, hours before Daniel's accident. Rebecca was back home by then.

19. As noted earlier, we are here as humans to further soul growth. Illness often occurs when we deny soul's needs. It was time for Samantha to begin the process of awakening to True Nature. Areas of our body that resist the soul consciousness can develop dysfunction depending on the needs of our soul. Drugs also contribute to body dysfunction.

:-)

~ 10 ~
The Aftermath

Fond memories of Easter egg hunts and a fun atmosphere, created by Rachel after Abigail's birth, rule the holiday after Daniel's death. Most of the family shares Easter while missing past celebrations. They want this day to fill with happiness and fun activities as well. Samantha takes many pictures and later sees the first evidence of what she believes to be orbs, signs of nearby spirits.

Guided to search the phenomenon on the Internet, she discovers a web site with much needed information (psychicinvestigators.net). Samantha also verifies intuition upon reading books by John Edwards who notes, there is indeed a life beyond this one. Yes, the ability to receive and send messages from the Otherside is real.

Now Samantha cries throughout the day while James works. She doesn't know that Daniel's death will help her to wake-up to who she, who we, really are. She thinks only of the last time she saw Daniel and believes her action to have him was selfish. Perhaps she should have remained mother's helper, continuing to watch her brothers and sisters as Mom earned a living by watching other peoples' kids. Maybe that's why God took him away.

Sometimes Daniel's spirit breaks through her grief. A smiley face appears etched into the side frame of the bathroom window screen one day. She soon sits on the toilet, whenever grieved, to look at the smiley face. Although feeling a bit odd to talk with him there, it becomes easier as Daniel's spirit communicates. Daniel's voice speaks inside her mind as she looks at the face with delight. It's a comforting reminder that her sunshine spirit is still around. She decides he allocates much time to be in-between worlds to visit loved ones.

Rachel, reeling in shock with the sudden death of her husband, deals with news reporters. The largest South Florida newspaper quickly publishes an account of Daniel's accident. He hit the rear of a car, it notes, trying to change lanes while driving his Suzuki Hayabusa motorcycle on the Interstate. A local paper reports that Daniel's Chinese-made motorcycle could travel at high rates of speed. There's no doubt in Samantha's mind that Daniel pushed his motorcycle to the limit. "Take it to the Limit," by the Eagles, was one of their favorite songs.

Samantha emails helpful Internet web site links to Rachel, hoping they'll help Abigail deal with Daddy's death. Spurred forward by Daniel's soul, she offers to visit. A depressed and distraught Rachel emails back to admit that she also communicates with Daniel. She invites Samantha for a visit.

Watching Rachel and Abigail deal with the challenges of an unwanted lifestyle becomes difficult upon arrival the following week. But Daniel's spirit supports them as they grieve. Samantha is there to help Rachel and herself deal with guilt over his death. Daniel's spirit prompts Samantha to show Rachel only unconditional love. She's ecstatic to sense him and does everything possible to keep his presence near.

Samantha says things without knowing why. She apologizes for their stormy relationship, especially during the past year.

"You're so precious to me," she says sincerely. "And I'm so very grateful to you for bringing Abigail into the world."

She knows it wasn't easy for Rachel to give birth to a child at forty-years-old. And she's thankful that Rachel did it with great anticipation and love, being careful not to smoke, drink, or do anything to detrimentally affect Abigail's development. Samantha stresses the vital role Rachel played in helping Daniel to get Home.

She notes it was part of their contract to bear his only child before physical death.

Rachel's face shows fleeting hints of recognition as she listens while perched on a wooden kitchen stool.

Daniel, Samantha explains, knew it was his destiny to help her have Abigail. There were several times when girlfriends could have bore him a child but Daniel refused to be a father. He knew, subconsciously, that he would not be there to help raise his child. He knew what it was like to grow up without a father and did not want that to happen to any child of his. He adored Abigail and never wanted to leave her.

Rachel looks confused to hear that souls wisely plan their earth life before birth. She listens as Samantha notes how carefully she chose Daniel's name to give them a clue as to his destiny.

No one is to blame for his death, Samantha stresses adamantly. He met his destiny, with Rachel's help, and that's a good thing.

It won't be easy for Rachel to live in the home bought less than eight months before Daniel's death. Samantha knows, by her own experience, and Rebecca's, it's not easy to raise a child without a father. She voices gratitude for the strong role Rachel continues to play caring for Abigail.

Family members hold memories, pictures, family videos, cassette tapes, presents, and cards given to them by Daniel. Rachel keeps everything accumulated over the course of a twelve-year relationship. His ashes and other things now serve as constant reminders. Yet, Samantha fails to see this as a blessing. She doesn't thank Rachel for keeping his things.
[20]

"Being with Rachel and Abigail," Samantha thinks while carefully watching Abigail, and ignoring her rigorous medication schedule, "is very difficult."

Rachel talks endlessly on the telephone. Samantha keeps trying to stop her from feeling guilty about Daniel's death. His accident, she continues to note between calls, was preordained. It's a knowing, not a hunch.

Samantha rarely ventures to the other end of the house, where the guest room remains empty, for in her mind, it belongs to Joy. Grateful to be with Rachel and Abigail, she doesn't care about suffering through small inconveniences. Intense pain fills her body but she believes it's justified as they sleep together in Daniel and Rachel's new king size bed. She remains quiet even though she thinks it odd to sleep on Daniel's side.

Daniel's soul remains near. Sometimes her new camera refuses to work when she tries to take pictures. She finally senses Daniel doesn't want her to take certain pictures. He seems in constant contact, using non-verbal communication (NVC). She's unfamiliar with the term NVC but later recognizes the phenomena after reading books on the subject by Robert Monroe. She calls it mental telepathy.

Intuition tells Samantha it's time to learn the lessons of forgiveness and patience. Samantha is there for Rachel, not for Abigail. She remains silent, many times, when she would otherwise have spoken. Abigail seems distant. She's not acting as when Samantha watched her alone. It's difficult to refrain from holding Abigail, singing to her, and rocking her as in the past. Samantha tries hard to establish a new relationship but memories hold her back.

Daniel prompts her to look in his beloved work truck on their third day together. Rachel agrees to let her search it. The climb into his truck is slow for it hurts to raise her knees. Trying to ignore the pain, she climbs up on the floorboard to lift her overweight body into the passenger seat.

Daniel's presence is strong when the truck's silver door closes behind her. She's grateful to feel him nearer. With now closed eyes, she'd bet her life that he's right there in human form. But she has no idea what to look for. Holding back tears, she looks around the seats while talking out loud.

"Just tell me what to look for," she asks the ethers.

Clear words fill her mind.

"Look inside the glove box."

A bulky, black case takes up most space inside the large storage area. It holds, she realizes with a sudden flash of recognition, his music CD's. Music has always been a big part of their lives. Samantha unzips the case to look through the CDs. Some of them are ones she repeatedly played in the 1970's when Daniel became interested in music. Daniel directs her to take the case home. Tears course down red cheeks upon leaving the truck while wondering if his presence will ever return so strongly.

She takes the CDs home the next evening, with Rachel's permission, after promising to return them the following week. The drive seems short, as she speeds down the turnpike, in a hurry to review the CDs to learn why she has them. James sleeps soundly as she enters the house so she moves quietly and closes the home office door behind her. She puts headphones on, and as music plays, is grateful to feel Daniel's presence again.

Daniel guides her by choosing songs for her to copy. His soul remains in transition choosing certain songs while she tries to hear them all. She soon realizes he's showing her, through music, his feelings before physical death. He wants her to know his state of mind when the accident occurred. Her goal, in making new CDs, is to believe that Daniel was miserable, for she feels better thinking he's now happy to be free. Daniel's goal is much different.

"No, not that one Mom," she hears. "Listen to the next song." Sometimes she hears, "Move on to the next CD."

There's a lot of misery in the music and it saddens her to hear it. Yet, uplifting songs, about Spirit and the Otherside, which she never thought would interest him, encourage her. Samantha copies songs as directed onto new CDs. She makes eleven CDs of songs Daniel listened to often in the months before physical death. The songs reflect both his state of mind upon physical death and state of being as his soul guides her to make them.

Samantha returns Daniel's CDs the following week. Rachel doesn't think Abigail knows her daddy has passed. But Abigail repeatedly goes around the corner outside to "talk to Daddy." At one point in the evening, Abigail and Samantha stand side by side in front of the sliding glass, den doors as Daniel's presence fills the room. They're watching Bruiser, the big, brown, pit bull puppy out on the back porch. Daniel got the puppy shortly before he passed away and Bruiser is now quite a handful for Rachel and Abigail to take care of.

Bruiser never acted this way before. Abigail and Samantha watch as he moans and growls, at the same time, with his nose pressed up against the sliding glass door. Samantha is certain Bruiser is communicating with them and it has something to do with Daniel.

Abigail and Samantha suddenly announce, in unison, "Yes, it's okay."

Abigail touches the window where Bruiser's nose sits as Samantha wonders why Bruiser is upset.

"It's okay Daddy," Abigail announces in a calm, grown-up voice.

Awe fills Samantha as a startled Rachel bolts up from the kitchen behind them. She sweeps Abigail into her arms as Samantha holds back tears. Bruiser seems very distraught, still trying to communicate. Samantha knows Abigail got the message for the child's power to connect with her daddy is strong. Samantha returns home the next morning.

Rachel telephones her days later to report Bruiser died suddenly. Rachel, Abigail, and Daniel's friend Jude took him out to run around county roads by the house. Bruiser collapsed at the side of the road. Abigail watched as the dog quickly died to be with her daddy. It was the second of several deaths Abigail would experience. [21]

Samantha feels guided to visit a used bookstore before returning for a third visit with Rachel and Abigail. She hasn't been there in a long time but knows there's a book to help her deal with Daniel's death. The clerk knowingly directs her to the requested book section and tells her to look at titles. In a self-assured voice, he notes books will choose her. She'll feel an undeniable urge to buy a book meant for her. She soon chooses six books including *Celestine Prophecy*, *Journeys out of the Body* and *Many Lives, Many Masters*. The store's owner lets her choose two more free books.

Three weeks before their annual family vacation, in the cabins at Bahia Honda State Park, Daniel directs Samantha to show family members the books. Each one, including Rachel, is to pick a book to read. They're to return books to read another book, if desired. Almost everyone chooses a book to read while on vacation.

The books Samantha reads help her to learn more about death, the afterlife, past lives, and destiny. While reading *Many Lives, Many Masters*, she gets the feeling that perhaps she's wronged Rachel, or Joy, in a past life. Samantha intuitively knows, this time, she must rectify the past to clear karma created in other lives. [22]

Daniel's spirit prompts Samantha to get out of bed, in the middle of the night, during her third stay at Rachel's house. He directs her through the breakfast nook and kitchen to his home office. "Daniel," she thinks remembering their habit of writing one another notes since he was ten-years-old, "might have written me a note before he died."

His last written communication was a series of faxes showing that James and Samantha could easily live nearby. Daniel read the daily newspaper and circled appropriate jobs so they could see there was work for them. He faxed them listings of houses for sale as well. Samantha, touched at the time, treasured the faxes and hoped they would soon be near one another again.

A pile of condolences catches her attention while sitting in his black leather chair trying to decide where to look. The number of communications amazes her even though she knows many people attended the funeral. She had no idea that so many coworkers and neighbors, from their old neighborhood, came to say goodbye. Samantha is also amazed to see notes from childhood friends. She wonders if Rachel sent them thank you cards.

Daniel's presence fills the room. Samantha begins to cry quietly in a state between grief and joy. He directs her to make copies of people's names that sent flowers, and cards, and of those who signed the book at the funeral home. She returns to bed, within an hour, after storing the list in her bag. Rachel and Abigail continue to sleep soundly.

In the morning, Rachel again jokes about Abigail's talks with Daddy. Abigail still goes outside, around the corner of the house, to "talk to Daddy." And now, she's demanding that Rachel place a plate of food at the dinner table, for he sits with them in his usual place. Abigail is a very insistent and perceptive two-year-old and Rachel puts the food on the table to please her. [23] She then thinks about taking Abigail to see a child psychologist.

Samantha makes the best use of what little time she has alone with Abigail. She tells her that Daddy Daniel and Nana will always be in her heart, in her blood, and nothing can ever change that. All Abigail need do is talk to Nana, in her mind, and she will hear her. Samantha doesn't understand why but words just flow from her lips.

Upon returning home, Daniel's soul directs her to type up Rachel's address on postal return labels. Samantha then sends thank you notes to many people on the list. Daniel wants them to know he cherished their time together. She's amazed at the specific messages he offers for friends. She signs every message, as if from Daniel's family, and is thankful to do something to help her son.

Visits to see Rachel and Abigail end the following week when Rachel finds the four sheets of paper Samantha gave Daniel to read two weeks before physical death. She telephones Samantha to tell her to never visit them again.

Now Samantha is even more depressed upon feeling the loss of Rachel and Abigail. She watches videos of their visits and notices static on the tapes. For the first time, static makes it hard to hear recorded sounds. The phenomenon continues to occur in subsequent family videos. (Static can be a sign of paranormal activity when videotaping.)

20. *Samantha's supposed loss is easier as Rachel now bears the burden of keeping his physical possessions. Gratefulness will be more common as Samantha realizes that Rachel's role is to help her awaken to the truth of BEing. Raising Abigail, while working a full time job, will not be easy for Rachel. With Daniel's prompting, Samantha will periodically encourage and thank Rachel for the wonderful job she does.*

Rachel's role in this game of life is of utmost importance to Samantha's increasing spiritual awareness. In essence as her spiritual friend and ally, Rachel agreed to play her difficult role because of their eternal love for one another. Rachel's valuable efforts, to help her learn the lesson of forgiveness, becomes clear in coming years. Samantha will realize that Rachel helped her to learn this most valuable lesson of human life.

Renard notes our "real life" depends on completely forgiving others. True forgiveness, Dr. Page reports, is the result of recognizing there's no separation "between ourselves and the person who has offended, for we are all one." Since we are in a dream world anyway, there really is nothing to forgive. There is One in which we live, and move, and have all BEing.

21. Samantha later consoles herself believing that Abigail, as we all do, chose life experiences before birth to help promote spiritual growth. It's common for souls to travel in the same group many times. Yet, the connection to Abigail does not feel as strong as that to Rebecca and Daniel. She knows the connection between Abigail, Rachel and Joy is much stronger.

Souls choose things to help them learn and grow with help from teachers and companions on the Otherside. Every aspect of soul's needs are profoundly studied before incarnation. Abigail's soul chose to learn about loss at a very early age. All three of Daniel's dogs moved on to the Otherside to be with him within ten months. Blind Sassy, the black malamute that had been with him for sixteen years, died quietly of old age before Christmas. Bear, the German Shepard, died the next year when his stomach turned upside down, living only a short time after a late night surgery. Compassion comes easily in later years as Abigail remembers what it's like to lose loved ones. She will learn other lessons at an early age as well.

22. *According to the teachings of Ernest Holmes, Karmic Law works through the Medium of the World-Soul. This mental tendency is both individual and Universal and the result of how humans use their mentality. Things that the individual sets in motion through the law ultimately "swing back" to the thinker.*

<u>Emmanuel's Book</u> *notes karma is really a mode of learning not "a balancing of books." Karma is a set of circumstances humans choose in each life they live "to find areas not yet in truth." We are the creators of everything happening to help us have experiences that propel our transformation back to the Light. No soul gives itself more work than it can do. There's a resolution to every experience, either through karmic action, or by the grace of God.*

"The very act of incarnation is the statement of a soul's yearning to become one again with the Light." We release karmic ties through our willingness to grow. After humans live many lives, it becomes possible to "put the

limited, doubting mind to the service of the heart." Humans seek Truth to finally return to the One in which we live, and move, and have all BEing.

    23. Several years later, information verifies that Abigail indeed sees her daddy at dinnertime. While listening to an audio version of <u>The Tibetan Book of Living and Dying</u>, Samantha learns that many entities still feel hunger for a number of weeks after death, including those who die suddenly, such as Daniel.

    The dead may not realize they are now out of their bodies. They often return to loved ones acting as usual and trying to communicate. Some require more time to recognize they are no longer in human form.

:-)

~ 11 ~
Woo, Woo Times

The telephone rings several times after Daniel's funeral but no one is on the line when Samantha picks up the receiver. The sound of static leaves her stumped, wondering if someone plays tricks on her. Later, she realizes other people experience after-death communications (ADCs). In a popular book, *Hello from Heaven*, authors note ADCs are spiritual gifts intended to increase spiritual awareness of who we are and why we're here. They also alert us to the truth, that there is no death and we all enjoy eternal love.

Daniel's spirit soon reports it's time to stop listening to the eleven CDs. The CDs served their purpose and now it's time to move on. Samantha weans the eleven CDs down to three with his guidance. She still listens to some of the original songs but begins to play the last three CDs more often. Daniel then directs her to stop listening to certain songs on those disks for they no longer reflect the awareness of his soul. Now she must make a memorial CD for family and friends.

The memorial CD holds inspiring songs related to his accident and the Otherside. They acknowledge there's no loss, no death. Samantha is surprised to hear "Inside Us All" by CREED. The song notes a piece inside everyone that helps them to carry on. Her awareness of that piece, in the heart's core, grows daily, as the song becomes her mantra.

The first year after Daniel's death is the hardest for Samantha's spiritual growth. Grief consumes her. Years ago, Daniel said her business efforts were a waste of time. He reversed his thinking months before physical death and told her to keep the business going. Focusing on work helped because it was something she could control.

Odd things continue to happen but Samantha usually

ignores them. The desktop computer that operated so perfectly before now makes work difficult. Samantha sits, with her back turned towards the windows, in the back corner of the home office, away from the door. She often sings while working. A strange thing happens, several times, when singing along to "I Miss You" by Sandra Pires. The song reminds her of Daniel. She sings as tears run down her face.

"I miss you. No one could take the place of you. No one could love me like you do."

The first few times she feels a presence, she stops singing, thinking James stands behind her. Yet, when she turns to greet him, no one is there. After searching the house several times in vain, she recognizes Daniel's presence. [24]

Just like everyone else, Rebecca and Samuel find it difficult to deal with Daniel's death. Rebecca feels Daniel's presence as well. She's now able to work but major medical issues continue to make life miserable. Samantha helps by picking Samuel up from school, several days a week, to watch over him until Rebecca' workday is done.

Driving during difficult times always makes Samantha feel better for she's in control of destinations. Now driving is even more enjoyable because Daniel's spirit usually surfaces when she listens to his memorial CD. One sunny day a small part of "Keep the Faith" by Bon Jovi starts to play erratically. The same words repeat over, and over, again.

"Mother, Father, there are things I've done I can't erase."

The words repeat for several minutes while Samantha becomes increasingly distraught. Tears run down her face as she hears Daniel asking for forgiveness. She wipes them away, with the back of her hand, so other drivers won't see them, and continues to drive.

"Stop it." She calls out forcefully to the air around her. "There is nothing to forgive."

The CD player switches to play another song. A

strong sense of relief fills her as she pats the passenger seat knowing Daniel's soul got the message.

Daniel's soul reaches out both day and night. When too tired to work, grief-filled Samantha sits in front of the television, to cry. The sound of the television drowns out her sobs. Daniel doesn't like the programs Samantha watches. One night, the television channel switches to MTV where a music video plays "The Power of Love." The television continues to switch channels on its own whenever she turns it on. Daniel guides her to watch late night comedy shows and notes, she needs to laugh, instead of fill her mind with doom and gloom. New programs change her mood considerably while laughing instead of crying.

Samantha often watches the video finished on the day of his funeral as well. One night, she repeatedly watches part of a Keys family vacation trip. Being the jokester that he was, Daniel planned to trick everyone with a huge, blackish, brown, plastic, palmetto bug. He attached the plastic bug to the door leading out to the view of the Bay in the morning. It was hard to miss since everyone went out that door. Some of them were frightened but they all had a good laugh. The fake palmetto bug remained a source of laughter throughout the day.

Bitter tears fall as Samantha thinks of their first family vacation without Daniel. After a while, she rises for a drink to get her through the night. A palmetto bug, just about the size of the one in the video, runs across her right foot as she turns on the kitchen light. She screams in terror. James jumps out of bed and runs into the kitchen. He chases the bug around the room and finally squashes it with his left foot.

This is the first of many palmetto bugs Samantha sees in the house over the next year. They appear every time she watches the video segment of Daniel's plastic palmetto bug. She finally stops watching the video but occasional bold ones appear in her kitchen, or living room, during times of great despair. Sometime later, Samantha learns it's Daniel's way of breaking through the veil to communicate.

Many times, bugs appear when James is gone. Samantha eventually learns to chase them herself. She kills and flushes them down the toilet at first. But then she begins to think she's to let them live. They're messengers sent by Daniel's soul to let her know he's still around. She is to treat them with love.

Samantha starts to speak with them in her mind. She thanks them for coming and says they belong outside and she'll release them without harm. All they need do is be still to be picked up and carried outside. She uses paper towels to scoop them up and is amazed that they let her. Upon seeing this new method, James really wonders about her sanity.

Depressed after midnight one night, she opens the kitchen cupboard to get a cup for ice cream. A palmetto bug quickly jumps onto her chest. She panics immediately, screams, and brushes it onto the floor. James is fishing in the Everglades so she's alone. She begins to cuss angrily at Daniel out loud.

"This isn't funny," she says stomping her feet up and down on the linoleum floor.

"Oh, come on Mom," Daniel replies quickly with a broad smile. "Lighten up. You have to admit it is."

Samantha sees him laughing in her mind. He thinks it's funny because he scared her more than he did while in the Keys. It's his way of letting her know he's still around. She isn't happy about the way he does it and asks him to find other ways to alert her of his presence. Daniel tells her to stop grieving for he wants her to be happy. He wants her to have some fun for a change. She agrees to try and then makes a new rule. She only wants to see certain creatures. The preferred list starts out as only butterflies, birds, and cats but soon expands.

The rest of the family tries to stop grieving as well. Rebecca proudly graduates from community college with great sadness. The day is spectacular with scattered clouds, in a bright blue sky, contrasting the green, finely manicured lawn. Samantha stands in the crowd on the lawn, with Samuel and Terrance, who just dyed his brown hair a hue of red orange. The perfect temperature hints of heat as they mass tightly into the throng of people.

 Graduates file by in what seems a never-ending line. Samantha fights back tears while looking for her beautiful, short daughter. She knows Rebecca's graduation is a bittersweet experience without her brother. Daniel and Rebecca dropped out of high school before graduating, just like their mother. They also got their equivalency diploma but did not wait as long as Samantha did to get it. Daniel followed his little sister's lead and got his equivalency diploma years after her. Rebecca finished the requirements for her associate's degree at age twenty-nine and now cannot stop thinking of Daniel. None of them can.

 Samantha knows Daniel is with them. A stranger soon verifies feelings. She spots Rebecca, wearing 'that' fake smile, in front of a tall, younger blonde-haired woman. The all too familiar smile says, "I'm pleased with myself but cannot be happy because Daniel is gone."

 "There she is," Samantha yells as Rebecca moves among people a foot, or more, taller.

 A stranger's voice fills the air, "Even though you're the shortest person, you're ten feet tall today," he announces loudly as Rebecca strolls past.

 Samantha knows, with all of her broken heart, that the words come from Daniel. The experience gives her new insight, knowing that God indeed works in mysterious ways. God works through stranger's words, angels, and other unseen beings. God also works by putting thoughts into our minds that we would never have known on our own. We are never alone. We need only ask God's help to get it.

 Other things happen to alert Samantha of Daniel's presence. Sometimes Daniel comes to take Samantha to his daughter. In Samantha's mind, she sees Abigail with Daniel in the wee hours of the morning. She seems to fly with him to Rachel's house. Samantha remembers flying over certain landmarks between their houses upon waking. After a few trips, it seems that she's in her room one minute and at Rachel's house the next.

Abigail always sleeps in bed with Rachel when they arrive. Daniel lovingly scoops Abigail out of bed and together they take her to the next room. He sits on his favorite, green, leather, Lazy Boy to hold Abigail in his lap. Samantha sits on the edge of the chair. As they rock, back and forth, Samantha strokes Abigail's long, light brown hair. And then she sings songs as when babysitting. Samantha seems to stay with them for a few songs before returning to her own bed.

The first Mother's Day without Daniel is tough to bear. Samantha begins work early, trying to update hiv nutrition handouts. But the computer refuses to install her camera software. The software helps her to print PDF files that are vital to the business. She soon sits quietly trying to decide what to do.

A sudden thought that she might have lost or deleted a necessary file surfaces. She opens the Windows Explorer to look at computer file names. One name grabs her attention and she clicks on it without thinking. A screen saver quickly covers the computer monitor.

"WE LOVE YOU MOM." It reads.

The pink letters scroll across a solid blue screen. Tears of grief and joy flow down plump cheeks as Samantha cries.

She finds it odd to find the file on Mother's Day. Daniel obviously hid it for her before physical death. The heartbreaking thought soon fills her with joy to know that his soul guided her to find it. She tries to remember when he could have changed the screen saver. In a short time, she learns he made the file months before physical death.

Daniel and Rachel had come over after work to pick

up Abigail. They all planned to go out to dinner so Samantha left the room to change her clothes. The video camera was in her hand when she returned. Daniel sat at her computer desk as Rachel changed Abigail's diaper. She asked him what he was up to but he just smiled, got up, and led her out the door. Yes, God is always reaching out to us through other people!

Rebecca arrives to pick Samantha up minutes after she solves the mystery. They spend the rest of the day at Lydia's Mother's Day family gathering. It's the first time Samantha leaves the house for a social event since Daniel's death. She's happy to communicate with Lydia's mother, Hannah, who continues to undergo treatment for brain cancer.

24. More than three years later, as Samantha edits this section of the book, the radio begins to play "Heaven Knows" by Donna Summer. It was, at one time, a favored song. Her attention shifts, from typing to the song, when she hears, "Heaven knows it's not the way it should be and Heaven knows it's not the way it could be."

Those words mean more to Samantha now. Singing often offered relief from pain and grief and always makes her feel better. It's as if she's connecting to God sometimes when singing certain songs. Samantha doesn't believe in coincidences and knows the song played to let her know she's finally back on her soul's chosen path.

:-)

~ 12 ~
Family at Play

Daniel's family vacations, with heavy hearts, the following week. They all thought Daniel, Rachel, and Abigail would be with them when they made the reservations eleven months earlier. Now two rented cabins sit next to each other so most of the adults travel back and forth before lulling themselves to sleep with alcohol.

    Samantha feels Daniel's presence and is happy every time something odd happens. She no longer feels like videotaping family events, but since vacation fills with unexpected happenings, is glad to have brought the video camera.

    A majestic, blue sky, with puffy white clouds, greets them in the morning. Walking out the door to see a beautiful landscape feels great. Small waves cascade out in the blue-green ocean making the water appear rough for boating. They have eight days to fish and snorkel so it doesn't bother them today.

    As her family makes breakfast in the other cabin, Samantha stands looking for an outfit to wear from the left side of the closet. A soft plop catches her attention. A blue shirt from the right side of the closet now sits on the floor. Another shirt falls as she stoops to pick up the first. She senses Daniel's presence but shrugs it off thinking it's just her imagination. A pair of pants falls to the floor before Samantha stands. Now there's no doubt that Daniel's playful spirit is letting her know he's there. Daniel is fooling around as he usually did in human form.

"Please Daniel," she cries filled with emotion. "My back and hips are hurting so I'd appreciate it if you'd stop dropping clothes onto the floor."

The fire alarm goes off in the other cabin. Its shrill sound pierces the air, reminding her of another family vacation when Daniel, Rachel, James, and Samantha left everyone else to spend time in Key West, before Abigail's birth.

Samuel was upset to see them go but seemed happy when Samantha traded hats with him before climbing into the van. The weather was perfect. James and Samantha rented motorbikes in Key West so they could ride along with Daniel and Rachel on their motorcycle. A small breeze served to cool them as temperatures rose above 80 degrees. Scattered clouds shielded them from the sun's rays.

Samantha was happier than she had been in a long time. She felt lucky to spend more time with Daniel and to ride a motorbike alone for the first time. Confidence filled her after a few hours of riding the motorbike well. James followed Daniel and Rachel as she motored behind them. A strong gust of wind suddenly blew Samuel's hat off her head. She turned the motorbike around, without a second thought, to get the hat. As she neared it, she was relieved to see nothing disturbed it. It lay near the curb in the right hand lane of the two lane paved road.

Samantha drove at about fifteen miles an hour. She slowed the bike and reached out her left arm to scoop up the hat easily but quickly lost control of the motorbike. She panicked as it went down. Instead of turning the bike off, she turned the handlebar connected to the gas line, and gunned the motor, twice. Intense pain filled her right leg as it scraped across the paved roadway.

She finally stopped the motorbike after scrapping her leg half way down the block. Samantha didn't know it then but she'd vividly remember that road burn after Daniel's accident. She'd know, without a doubt, that his injuries were at least a thousand times more than hers on that day.

A police cruiser saw the accident and blocked traffic as Samantha turned the motorbike off. She assured the officers she was fine and got back onto the bike in shock. Her heart pounded erratically and her right leg burned badly but she didn't want to ruin her family's day. She blotted the blood that oozed from her right leg with tissues from her pocket as she drove. The police cruiser followed Samantha until she caught up to them. The 'accident' spoiled her plan to snorkel the next day, in the crystal blue waters of the Dry Tortugas.

Later at a small motel in the evening, Samantha admitted the pain in her leg was severe. They all went to a drug store where Daniel chose a cream that she applied liberally throughout the night. Everyone awoke to the piercing shrill of a fire alarm shortly before 3:00 AM. The deafening noise filled their room so they ran outside to get away from it. The sound was just as loud outside the building. They soon learned that a drunken prankster, returning from the local bar, set off the alarm just to have some fun.

Now the Key West trip fills her mind as she dresses and moves to the cabin next door. Everyone stands laughing as she enters the kitchen. The smoke alarm, they note in unison, went off without a reason. It continued to blare, for a short time, even after James removed the batteries. Samantha tells them it's Daniel's prank to let them know he's there. They all ignore her. It's an unexplainable event to them.

Samuel feels Daniel's loss strongly. He misses wresting and rough housing with him. Although not fully aware of it, this day becomes the first time Samantha acts as a channel.

"I wish Uncle Daniel was here to play games with me," Samuel notes with a frown.

A surge of energy rushes into Samantha's body.

"Would you like to wrestle with me?" She quickly asks grinning from ear to ear.

Samuel is glad to oblige her.

Samantha's body is in no condition for wrestling a young boy but that doesn't stop her as years filled with illness are forgotten. She holds more than 165 pounds on her 5' 2" frame even though she's lost a bit of weight. With no regard to a heart arrhythmia, obesity, high blood pressure, spinal conditions, or osteoarthritis she proudly stands before Samuel. Excitement fills the air as they tie their hair up like sumo wrestlers. Rebecca sets up the video camera to tape the action.

One-hundred-thirty pound Samuel lies on the floor begging for mercy in less than a minute. It's no small feat for Samuel is a strong boy.

"Ya ha, ya ha," Samantha says loudly. "That's what Daniel says."

Samuel looks at her strangely as she announces, "He'll always be with you."

"Why can't I have a normal Nana?" Samuel angrily shouts while easily pushing his way up from the floor.

He hurriedly rushes out the cabin door to get as far away from Samantha as possible. She looks at Rebecca and shrugs, not knowing what to say, for Daniel just interacted with Samuel while using her body. The possibility of channeling other spirits enters her mind. Hours later, she merrily squirts people with the water hose, laughs and runs up stairs, usually difficult to climb, as they yell. It's a typical 'Daniel prank.'

This is their first nine-day vacation and they plan to watch the sunset together, at least one night during their stay, from the old Bahia Honda Bridge. They scheduled a sunset event weeks before thinking Rachel would share Daniel's ashes to toss into the ocean. Lydia and Joseph soon arrive with friends to participate.

It's extremely windy for the first time in all the years

vacationed in the Keys. Fishing is nearly impossible so most of the adults drink instead. Some joke around as the uphill climb to the top of the old bridge begins. Samantha is among them. Samuel again asks for a normal Nana as her jokes touch upon spiritual topics. She then grumbles of aches and pains all the way up to the top of the hill.

Daniel's memorial CD is ready to play but there are no ashes to distribute. They say farewells to him anyway. Friends help to break the silence of grief. Someone else videotapes as Samantha mourns while looking in the distance at the bareness of their favorite island. Her heart feels as empty as the island remembering how they snorkeled there. Trees and mangroves have disappeared compliments of the last hurricane.

For the first time, Samantha sees colors and shapes, coming from the sun, when she finally takes her turn videotaping. Two white puffs move in line with the sun along with green and fuscia colored shapes. The sunset is spectacular with various shades of orange, yellow, purple, and pink. Colors appear throughout clouds as the sun moves below the horizon. As they watch it sink, Samantha apologizes to Samuel for not being a normal Nana. Samuel forgives her.

Windy conditions continue causing the family to spend more time together than ever before. When they venture out to the National Wildlife Refuge, Samantha finds herself channeling Aunt Deborah. Samantha relays a message to her mom who walks slowly with a cane. Deborah wants her sister to know how proud she is of her and glad to see her outside walking a nature trail, despite blindness and other medical conditions.

Everyone complains about the wind and blames their bad luck on timing. Many of them say it wasn't worth the trouble to tow the boat to the Keys. They could have stayed home and fished more where the wind isn't quite as strong. Samantha is the one to blame, as far as they are concerned, because she reserved the cabins.

Samantha is tired of taking the blame for things that go wrong. The next morning, she tells Terrance it's time for someone else to make the family's vacation plans.

"Well we can't control the wind," Terrance replies. "We're not God."

"Oh yes we are," Samantha replies quickly, "each and every one of us."

Terrance shakes his head in silence and hurries away.

Now, the entire family thinks Samantha is crazy. She ends the vacation video with "Only God Knows Why," a song Daniel's soul led her to record. It seems a fitting end to their first family vacation without him in physical form. His spirit flows beside her in the van as family pulls the barely used boat out of the water.

Later, while viewing a picture of Samuel on old Bahia Honda Bridge, she notices an unexplained bright, white circle of light. She recalls feeling Daniel's presence strongly then. Author James Van Praagh notes, spirits often show up as whitish spots, "lights" or "flashes" on photos. Samantha will soon recognize these oddities in other pictures as well.

:-)

~ 13 ~

More Time to Grieve

Grief leads Samantha to dedicate a web site to Daniel. She soon begins to write books about him to post there for Abigail. In time, the site changes to offer information to help people increase their awareness of God.

Samantha still thinks only of her loss and decides that the world consists of "us" and "them." People in the "us" category always seem to have health issues and hardship in the physical state. They teach others and learn life lessons. People in the "them" category have priorities like wealth and fame. In her mind, they are mainly selfish people who rarely change. Samantha decides her kids, herself, and a few familiar people are in the "us" category. But there are more people in the "them" group. She knows it sounds paranoid but believes it just the same. [25] James, Samantha believes, operates from the "them" consciousness. Still obsessed with fishing, he's alone less often after joining a fishing club. Samantha doesn't know that being in nature is a great way to connect with God.

James requests, for her to help financially support the household, continue. She now increases efforts to make money. Listening to Daniel's music, as she mourns, seems the best way to work. Samantha loves to help people deal with hiv by teaching them about good nutrition. She meets her goal by helping people learn that good eating habits lessen medication side effects. Short family outings help to get Samantha out of the house. The dysfunctional family's night out at the racetrack is always a good excuse to drink. She sinks deeper into the drama thinking only of her own pain when drunk.

Drama heightens as Samantha spends more time at her self-made Wailing Wall. The chalkboard with the smiley, sunshine faces hangs in the pantry but she cannot bear to look at it. She leans on the other side of the wall, where it stands, every night at midnight. Very quietly, sobs shake her fat body as she continues to mourn. Samantha feels as if every pore of her frame gushes out blood. And she begs God to let her die so she can be with her son. [26]

Everything experienced is part of her journey to spiritual awareness. When she learns about past life regression, she decides to try it. Samantha believes it's possible to learn why things happened as they did. Issues from a past life, she decides, continue. The feeling that she wronged Rachel and Joy in a past-life haunts her.

Samantha begins to lose interest in the hiv nutrition work. Editing the company newsletter is no longer a concern but she persists because Daniel told her to continue. Family notes the business is a waste of time and money. She decides to publish the newsletter for two more years, if she can bear to live that long.

Rebecca and Samuel need her and she wants to help Daniel's soul. Abigail, Samantha believes, needs saving from a life of misery that Rachel, Abigail, and herself suffered through during many lifetimes. She trusts Daniel to tell her what to do and hopes to find a way to make things better. Consuming thoughts of the child, needing her, surface after nearly a month of not seeing Abigail. She feels distanced but knows the girl still feels the bond Daniel helped to build. Despite appearances, their bond, like hers with Samuel, Rebecca, and Daniel will never be broken. She feels it in her gut and promptly decides to see someone to help her deal with past lives.

Daniel's spirit comes in dreams. Yet, she cannot communicate with him because every time she sees him, she cries. She has no idea that grief and sorrow affect how often spirits can break through "the veil" to communicate. Now it becomes difficult to sleep for she wakes often with tears streaming down her face. Both Rebecca and Terrance admit to seeing Daniel in dreams too. Terrance is shocked, while trying to sleep, to see his face floating near the ceiling fan.

Daniel's spirit continues to find ways to reach her during waking hours. It helps her deal with grief and helps Daniel's soul with unfinished business. One day she senses his presence and clearly hears his words. He asks her to contact Alfred, the man who tried to act as his father from the time he was ten-years-old.

Daniel reconnected with Alfred, after a lapse of more than fifteen years, just three months before physical death. He sent Alfred information about Samantha's newsletter. Alfred then contacted her by email asking about her business and they continued the correspondence. He learned of Daniel's death through an email that Ruth sent him.

Knowing the connection is important, Samantha quickly emails Alfred. He emails back with his telephone number so she phones him the next day. Alfred is surprised when she says Daniel wants them to talk. While shopping for a new home, he felt Daniel's presence in one preferred house. The presence of his close friend Rene, a psychic and medium now on the Otherside, accompanied Daniel. Alfred realized Daniel and Rene guided him to the house for Rene exactly described the kind of house he would live in years before physical death. He decided to buy it because of their presence but became disappointed when the sense of them left.

Samantha tells Alfred that Rebecca, Terrance, and she all feel Daniel's presence. Rebecca and Terrance wonder if they just imagine Daniel and Samantha doesn't feel his presence as much as before. Alfred delights her because he also senses Daniel and doesn't call her crazy.

Alfred, a court appointed guardian for wayward boys, then tells her how he met Daniel. Daniel's friends dropped him off because he was high on drugs. They didn't know what else to do with him. Alfred began to take an interest in Daniel's welfare. He learned that Daniel spent a lot of time caring for Rebecca since Samantha went to college during the day and worked at night. Alfred then helped ten-year-old Daniel by caring for three-year-old Rebecca so Daniel could have some time to be a child.

Samantha hadn't known the extent of Daniel's drug addiction the last time Alfred saw him. Weeks later, she mails Alfred a copy of the videotape made of Daniel. She thanks him for sharing a part of his life with them and for helping Daniel to grow. Then she lets him know that a Dale Carnegie course, taken as part of a construction manager's job, changed Daniel's outlook on life. Daniel made positive changes and seemed to know that his lifetime was ending. Alfred is relieved to hear Daniel's life improved.

Odd hours continue to separate Samantha from the world. Much of the business is Internet based and it's easier to work late at night with the dial-up connection so she often works until 3:00 AM. Other things capture her time during daylight hours.

Samantha soon cherishes many memories of Daniel's spirit as it begins to accompany her in the wee hours of the morning. Before bedtime, she sits on the carpet facing the sliding glass doors in the dining room, looks out into the back yard, and waits for some sign of Daniel.

The presence of deceased family members fills the room every night. Sometimes they offer gifts as she looks beyond the yard at the empty manicured lot behind the house. Golden balls of light appear by the backyard tree. They move slowly toward her as she watches in delight. She's not afraid. In fact, she's still begging God to let her be with Daniel. Samantha hears Daniel's voice as the orbs of golden light move through sliding glass doors.

"Take the light into your heart Mom," he says. "Take the light into your head."

Increased tranquility fills Samantha with each ball of light scooped into her hands to place into her head or heart. "Perhaps," she thinks, "life must be accepted without judgment or question." Now a firm believer in reincarnation,

Samantha feels her life lessons are to learn forgiveness and patience. She has no idea what forgiveness really means but a strong sense notes her life's goal is near.

Possessing little knowledge about regression, she tries to learn of past lives by meditating while using information in Dr. Weiss's book. The few fragments received convince her, she's on the right track. In one sequence, a freckle-faced, young, Irish girl in a castle runs from a fire. Many other people run the other way. She's the sole survivor. Now Samantha thinks she has to "save them all." She also senses her children and knows what the outcome of their lives will be. Fragments of past lives make sense and their current life deals with the same issues faced in previous lives.

After recalling more past lives, she decides to see a credentialed Hypnotherapist. It seems almost too easy to find one specializing in past life regression. The medical professional holds several academic degrees and needs permission from Samantha's doctor, along with a written prescription for a medical diagnosis. Three incurable conditions and a long list of other illnesses make it easy to meet requirements.

Surprisingly, the Hypnotherapist is in the same medical complex as her doctor of fifteen years. Samantha soon recalls being a five-year-old, Irish girl, in a castle that's set on fire by the "Scots." Everyone in the castle tries to get away from the fire. Many of them are now in her current family. The red-haired, Irish girl runs against the stream of panicked people. They all think she's crazy for telling them there's a safe way to the outside.

"Follow me," she cries. "I know the way out."

No one follows her as she runs through a secret door in the castle wall. She escapes the fire alone. They all run the other way to burn. Samantha tells the Hypnotherapist she now has to "save them." She feels tears rolling down her face but is not emotionally upset. The therapist ends the regression.

Samantha remembers recalling the past life but the $175 session is worth it, even though not covered by insurance. It verifies that she can do past life regression on her own. She decides to do more regressions when not tired and less likely to affect results.

Beliefs quickly change. Now she believes souls are reborn into physical bodies and often travel with the same souls. There are lessons to learn in each life. It's time to pass on to a new body upon learning lessons. Sometimes, if a soul isn't ready to enter a physical body, its spirit will do other things. Souls, as Daniel, may stay between planes of existence to take care of unfinished business.

Samantha thinks she can help Daniel's soul continue on its journey and leave the transition state. There's a strong sense that he's between realms trying to protect his daughter, and offer his family comfort. Her heart aches for Abigail. Her arms long to hold her, to comfort, and tell her she is loved beyond anything she now might feel.

By most human eyes, Abigail appears to have lost most of her family. Since her daddy's death, she seems stuck in a sea of negativity, never seeing his side of the family. Samantha knows everyone in the physical state has a special role to play. In the grand scheme of things, there's only so much she can do for Abigail. [27]

Samantha remains locked into the "us" and "them" way of thinking. She still refuses to open up to greater possibilities. But she remembers words to one of the songs on Daniel's CDs. "… just believe in who we are and nothing else matters…open mind for a different view…" [28]

A casual relationship begins to change in June when Mary emails a web site link to Isaiah and Priscilla, a couple helping people connect with past lives and departed loved ones. The so-called coincidence fosters a friendship between Mary and Samantha, increasing their self-awareness.

Samantha's quest for enlightenment continues as she finds answers to constant questions by searching the Internet.

An unseen hand chooses links to follow. Useful web sites, about understanding spirituality, guide her thoughts. Information helps greatly while celebrating Rebecca's thirtieth birthday and Terrance's fortieth. Both birthdays are milestones without also bearing the loss of a loved one.

Samantha notices spirit orbs and white noise, the same sporadic static in videos of visits with Abigail and Rachel, while viewing the party video. It's also in later family tapes and seems a common occurrence amid hearty guffaws of laughter.

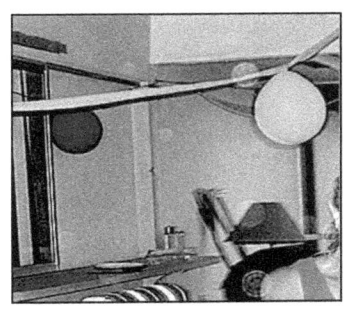

25. Race-consciousness often plays a major role in human life. Earth is the only place where souls grow spiritually. But as noted by Dr. Page, humanity exists within the Quantum Hologram, organized into patterns or form, through the power of intention or thought. Within this hologram, we move through experiences to see what it's like so we'll know. Everything on earth promotes separation. We believe in duality and differences such as good and bad, pain and pleasure, light and dark. But there are no differences when we wake-up from this dream world. There's nothing to separate us from each other. We are the same in every respect, One, having never left our Father.

Within the Oneness of God, only Love exists. But humanity lost its way many, many, eons ago to experience duality, forgetting the True Self. New souls continue to enter the consciousness of earth to help raise human awareness. Doctors diagnose some of these misunderstood souls as having "medical conditions" such as Autism and ADHD. Many more souls coming to earth are now more aware of their telepathic, whole-brain thinking. Unlike most humans, they are not insisting on breaking everything down into a language that makes no sense to collective thinkers.

Samantha will soon know, without a doubt, that we are all part of the One – unique mind-bodies in different states of awareness – but the same in essence, perfect, whole, and complete within God.

26. Things begin to make sense as Samantha puts the puzzle pieces together, realizing her propensity to replace the God within. The sun, a symbol of God, worshipped in previous lives, is vital to her awakening.

Daniel was her sunshine boy from the day he was born. When Rebecca gave birth to Samuel, Samantha called him her sunshine boy. It was hard to forget 27-year-old Daniel's reaction when he first heard her refer to Samuel as sunshine boy for they were his treasured words.

Unemployed Daniel needed money so Samantha paid him to fix things around the house. Samuel arrived just as Daniel finished his task. Samantha excitedly opened the den door.

"Hello my sunshine boy!" she said letting Samuel in.

"I thought I was your sunshine boy Mom," Daniel noted filled with surprise.

"You're my sunshine man now Daniel," Samantha replied.

Daniel's hurt look before he turned his head quickly away was hard to miss.

27. Abigail chose her earth life to include the best mother (before coming into human form) just like everyone else. It's common for souls to travel in the same group many times and there's no deeper relationship on earth than that of a mother and child. Father's were mothers too and once connected there is never separation. There is always Oneness even when we choose not to share a physical life. Meeting one another in dreams is common. Samantha knew Abigail met her father in dreams and during waking hours. Samantha counted on that relationship to offer Abigail any help she might need.

28. It will be some time before Samantha realizes that terms like "us" and "them" are just more ways the ego uses to keep us thinking we are in a body. It's all about separation for the ego. The ego's method of dealing with unconscious guilt and fear is to project it onto others.

As Renard notes, "Whenever you respond to your ego you will experience guilt, and you will fear punishment." The ego represents a delusional system, and speaks to it creating a whole new level. This delusional level is a thought system of sin, guilt, fear, attack, and defense. It can be acted out "to protect your seemingly separated mind, which you think of as your soul, from your terrible, yet completely unconscious guilt and fear."

:-)

~ 14 ~
New Life Begins

Daniel's sudden departure exacerbates family circumstances, such as medical conditions and lifestyle changes. Rebecca, Ruth and Samantha deal with disease while Terrance deals with new issues. Now accustomed to a diagnosis of multiple sclerosis, he considers divorce and life as a gay man. A new life will soon begin.

Samantha continues to plan days and nights based on health issues and medication schedules. Volunteer work and editing the company's newsletter keeps her busy. Samuel is out of school for the summer so she gets him from camp every day. It forces her out of the house, leaving less time to grieve.

Family and friends fear for Samantha's mental health. Many refer to her as crazy Nana.

"Daniel is dead and he's not talking to anyone," they all say repeatedly.

"Perhaps," Samantha thinks when Daniel communicates, "What they say is true."

She believes Isaiah can help to set her human mind at ease but is not quite ready to see him, or to focus on spirituality. Strange unexplainable things continue to occur. Samantha totes the portable CD player to the car so she can listen to Daniel's memorial CD while driving. But it acts erratically. Songs on the CD refuse to play normally even after she cleans the player. Sometimes the player pauses or repeats certain words. She thinks Daniel communicates through his favorite songs. A memorable experience occurs in mid-June.

Samantha bought an insurance policy when Daniel was seven-years-old. She never expected him to die before she did but purchased it as a favor for a friend. The woman's husband needed to make a monthly quota to keep his new job. Daniel's MetLife policy cost only $16.34 a year for $1,000 of coverage. Since it was a whole life policy, she could cash it in for a certain amount of money at any time. It seemed like a good investment. In later years, it also seemed silly to let the policy lapse so she continued to pay for it. MetLife restructured the company and offered shares to certain policyholders the year before Daniel died. Samantha received thirteen shares of MetLife stock.

Now after Daniel's death, she decides to get the insurance money for Abigail, even after his presence says she won't need it.

"Don't you remember Mom?" Daniel asks patiently. "I told you. I had good life insurance. The house will be paid off and there will be enough money for Abigail and Rachel to live well."

Stubborn Samantha still insists on investing. When she gets the insurance check, she decides to visit a MetLife representative. A beautiful cloudless day makes the drive to his office easier. Pretty, blue skies accompany perfect temperatures as she fights back tears. The song *"Hang Tough"* plays repeatedly as she motors down tree-lined streets. Samantha feels blessed upon realizing that what she suspected is indeed true. Daniel's spirit breaks though the veil of illusion to get her undivided attention through music.

A huge, very colorful, Indian statue sits in the MetLife representative's office. Samantha feels an unexplainable bond with this kind man as he talks about how it got there. Like a runaway train barreling down mountain roads, emotions soon take control, while speaking of Daniel's death. The man consoles her throughout their forty-five minute meeting. He agrees to open an account, without a fee, as long as the money remains untouched for at least ten years. At the end of their meeting, he rises from his brown, leather, executive chair, shakes her hand, and says, "Stay tough. Daniel is still around."

She hasn't mentioned the *"Hang Tough"* song and wonders how he can know such a thing. A river of tears cascades down red cheeks while walking to the car. She jerks the car door open as sobs convulse her throat.

Her hands shake making it difficult to start the car. The key refuses to fit properly into the ignition. Samantha stops trying, turns on the CD player, and tries to start the car again. This time it roars to life. She starts to back out of the parking spot but notices the CD has not started to play. It begins the second she looks at the player to make sure it's on. The player skips over the first several tracks on the CD, as she watches in delight. It then begins to play "Silent Lucidity" by Queensrÿche. Sensing Daniel's presence, she concentrates on the words of the song.

"Hush now don't you cry. Wipe away the teardrop from your eye. You're lying safe in bed. It was all a bad dream spinning in your head. Your mind tricked you to feel the pain of someone close to you leaving the game, of life."

A combination of extreme joy and human grief consumes her. It's the first of many times Daniel's soul embraces her in such a way.

Days later, Rebecca, Lydia, Hannah, and Samantha leave for Florida's West coast. Hannah's cancer treatments are over. She hasn't seen the Mystery Train Dinner Theatre so Lydia decides to take her. The foursome leave Lydia's house on Saturday planning to return the next day. There's little time to relax for the short twenty-four hour trip is much too quick for either Hannah or Samantha to enjoy.

"Take it Easy" by the Eagles plays as Rebecca drives. Samantha senses Daniel as a motorcycle drives quickly up from the left lane. It changes lanes, to zip effortlessly in front of them, before zooming out of sight. The rider looks like Daniel and wears a shirt with the familiar "No Fear" logo. He's reminding her to let go of fear.

"Daniel is free, happy, and wants us to be happy too," she says to deaf ears.

This is bald-headed Hannah's last holiday for she's in the final stages of brain cancer. A two-inch scar on the side of her head serves as a surgery souvenir. Tiny tufts of hair are barely visible near the scar.

   The older women talk after the dinner show when their daughters leave for the bar. Hannah asks questions about spiritual experiences. Most questions are of paranormal things Samantha just learned. Hannah is especially interested in learning if she can return to her family after physical death. Samantha happily answers queries, fearlessly and honestly, as they sit by an outdoor swimming pool.

   Daniel's presence again graces them during the drive back to Fort Lauderdale. An unexplainable diamond shape seems to come out of nowhere as Samantha videos clouds. A round, pinkish light appears directly in front of her for about thirty seconds. She is joyous to sense Daniel's presence but feels he has not yet found peace. Perhaps, he remains between worlds, between lives, and will for a long time. She hopes the thought is untrue.

   Divine providence offers verification of her wayward thoughts days later after retrieving the record player from a local repair shop on July 3. An unfamiliar, very old, 45-rpm record falls to the floor as she starts to put the player back on a shelf. The names on the record are hard to read. She has no idea where it came from. Its title is "When it's Time to Go."

   Although the record houses a large scratch, it plays flawlessly but it's not her type of music. "This," she thinks with great apprehension, "is a sign that Daniel's spirit is getting ready for its next level." It concerns her greatly that all the things his spirit does to help them get over his death might stop. Tomorrow is July 4, 2004, exactly three months since his transition and the thought of a different kind of Independence Day for Daniel causes great sadness. Samantha is not ready to let him go.

   Independence Day is hard on the entire family for they always celebrate the day with Daniel. Several things alert Samantha of his presence. An orb drifts away from Rebecca as she jokes and a mist seems to come from her cup on the counter. Rebecca now drinks Daniel's favorite alcohol, Jack Daniels.

Jeremiah becomes the topic of discussion. Lost in his own grief, Jeremiah is not reaching out and now the family has stopped trying to contact him. Daniel's death plagues him because he thinks if he'd only done something different Daniel would still be alive. The thought mirrors their beliefs.

Today's gathering ends before dark making it the first year the family does not watch fireworks together. Blasts of brilliant light fill the sky as they deal with loss alone. Samantha sleeps in her home office for by this time she rarely sleeps with James. Occasionally, she looks through windows to see fireworks from small cities nearby. The knowing that there will never be another Fourth of July with Daniel consumes her. She falls asleep with a book in her hand after midnight.

Something wakes her hours later. The word "cat" fills the air as she listens intently. A joyful smile now graces her lips in recognition.

Upon hearing the word, while working in her office several weeks earlier, she knew Daniel found a new way to communicate. Samantha was crying the first time she heard the sound. She stopped crying, wiped tears, and listened for the sound again. The word "cat" seemed to come from the closet. Samantha slowly slid the louver door open and heard "cat" repeated several times. She knew where the sound came from upon spotting Abigail's toy telephone on a shelf. Samantha picked up the toy to see it was on.

The telephone is one of Abigail's favorite toys to play with when visiting. It has six buttons and a dial to spin at the bottom. Each button has a picture and the spinning dial holds four different pictures. The telephone identifies them with the push of a button or spin of the dial.

Samantha didn't know what to think so she just put

the telephone back on the shelf and closed the closet door.

Later, she thought the toy acted oddly because the batteries were old so she put new batteries in it. But the word "cat" sounded throughout the room whenever she thought of Daniel. When she turned the toy off, it seemed to come on by itself.

Samantha, now used to the toy acting oddly, feels comforted to know Daniel's soul is still around and falls back asleep. She will soon learn that God works through spirits, humans and animals.

As usual the next morning, James remains silent, unable to share feelings. He seems unaffected by Daniel's death and never speaks of him. James finally shares a dream of Daniel telling him he wasn't dead.

"I told him," James says with a smirk, "to go away because he was dead. I saw him in his casket."

James is very fond of cats and the next day kittens come to the back porch. A bold, orange-striped kitten is the first to arrive. Two more kittens come days later. [29]

Every morning and night James sits with the kittens to talk. The three pharaoh cats are afraid of people but are happy to eat out of his hand. They get nervous when he tries to pet them but canned cat food always brings them near. James names the bold, orange kitten Bart and the others Wylie and Casper.

Samantha is glad to see James care for and talk to them. She knows the kittens are not for her. Bart is the only one that looks at her from several feet away. The other two run upon seeing her. Rebecca also knows Daniel sent the kittens. She tells Samantha her brother always said he wanted to be a cat in his next life. Samantha doesn't think humans can regress but knows the kittens are there for a reason. Days after their arrival, she tells James Daniel sent him the kittens. James still thinks she's crazy.

It was hard for James to train their other cats to use a cat door to enter the back porch. Constant night raids, by local raccoons, forced him to move the door a foot higher, so now it's even harder for animals to use. Surprisingly, all three kittens use the cat door without any training.

Their older, gray cat Missy accepts the kittens easily. She seems to enjoy Bart's company. Missy has seen many cats come and then die, leaving her alone. Many of Missy's own kittens died and others left the porch never to return. Batman, a sleek and beautiful black feline, Rebecca's first cat, lived to be 20-years-old. He died one morning as James held him the year before. Daniel and Rachel then gave him a cat but a neighbor ran over her a month after Daniel died.

At the end of June, Daniel's soul tells Samantha the world is changing. She is to cash in the government savings bonds held for Abigail and Samuel. The value of these bonds will not be as much as expected and will continue to lessen. Samantha does as directed. It's the first of many communications alerting her to future world events.

Depression worsens but she senses a need to stay more in her spiritual self. It's much too depressing to focus on the human state. Samantha wants to help Daniel and Abigail but fears there's nothing she can do for Abigail. She now avoids work, lived for since her kids left home, and begins to watch family videos more often.

Her intuitive friend Mary contacts her by email. Their friendship deepens when Mary asks Samantha to join her and another friend for a session with Isaiah and Priscilla. Mary arranges the meeting and notes the cost for individual work is $95 a session. It sounds like a bargain to Samantha after visiting the costly Hypnotherapist.

The session with Mary, her friend Tela, and Samantha goes well. Isaiah notes Samantha has lots of past-life experience in metaphysics and spiritual areas. He hints that they'll be able to do good work, both in and out of the body, which will be helpful for everyone. The thought excites Samantha but she notes money is a big issue. He's certain they can work out an agreeable fee.

Samantha wants to help Daniel pass out of transition, if that's his wish. It troubles her to feel his presence much less now. The subject of channeling interests her. Samantha is relieved to know that Isaiah can channel. He wants to teach her how to do it alone, instead of depending on him. Although she's anxious to see him again, it's almost two months before she finally does.

Excuses rise every time Isaiah schedules an appointment. Prescription medications, along with bladder and bowel issues, make it hard to plan excursions. She stopped trying to work a "regular job" ten years before because of increasing disease. Declining health now seems to require more time every day and she refuses to leave the house before 11:00 AM.

It's hard to explain what happens around her. Samantha keeps hearing Daniel, telling her to call Rachel, but hesitates even though she misses her and Abigail. Daniel's soul succeeds in getting Samantha's attention despite her refusal to contact Rachel. Strange noises erupt one day. She tries patiently to find their source. It's clear that they come from the pantry when she opens the door and a can of soup falls to the floor. Several other cans sit near the blackboard with the treasured smiley faces. Samantha cries sensing Daniel's presence and immediately pushes feelings aside to telephone Rachel. When the answering machine comes on, she leaves a message asking how everything is. Daniel directs her to keep leaving monthly telephone messages. She is also to continue sending Abigail the monthly cards started last year.

Samantha cries with joy knowing, without a doubt, that Daniel communicates more now than ever before. As she reads *Transformed by the Light*, by Dr. Melvin Morse, she's grateful to know that other people are guided from the Otherside. It comforts her to talk with Mary about the 'woo woo' things that happen. Mary never calls her crazy and, in fact, does everything she can to calm Samantha's fears. Everyone else continues to ignore Samantha while gossiping about how crazy she is.

Shortly after Samantha's call, Rachel begins to drop by James' workplace so he can see Abigail. Samantha is thankful that Rachel reconnects with someone. James begins to see them regularly and reports that they're doing well. Sometimes he takes them to lunch when Rachel is in town and sometimes James visits them at their house. Samantha senses she is not to interfere or push to see them herself.

29. A Course in Miracles notes, the ego is against communication, which is controlled by the ego's need to protect itself. The ego disrupts communication when it feels threatened. Opening our heart to others including animals, the environment, or through community work is an opening to love.

Emmanuel notes, "The purpose of human love is to awaken love for God." Sometimes one may think they're in love but instead are immersed in the physical body and human ego. The relationship between James and Samantha lacked the closeness of friendship. Cats would become James's confidants.

Four years later, while reading Destiny of Souls by Michael Newton, Samantha is certain that Daniel's spirit guided the kittens to help James. "Pets have the capacity to lift our spirits and foster healing while providing us with love and companionship without reservations." Animal souls are not ego-driven so identity issues do not overwhelm them. Humans can learn from them as they accept and blend with their environment.

:-)

~ 15 ~

Spirit Contacts

Rebecca and Samantha continue to sense Daniel's presence. As friends speak of departed loved ones, Samantha consoles them by explaining a new perception of death. Their family, just like hers, will rejoin in other lives. Daniel, she says, was with her in past lives and will be again. Opening her mind to move into unknown territory often scares her but she knows things happen for a reason. Everyone, she feels, subconsciously knows of past lives. It's just a matter of opening the mind to different ideas. Everything is preplanned based on lessons taught or learned. A belief in reincarnation strengthens while sending web site links on spirituality, and the Otherside, to friends and family.

Family and friends are not pleased with her increasing spirituality. Only Rebecca tries to understand. Samantha often senses resistance in people when explaining her new beliefs. They cross their arms and stare at her, as if she's crazy. People, Rebecca often reminds her, are entitled to their own beliefs.

"Be careful, other people won't understand channeling or the telepathy we share," she says sternly with a shake of her finger.

Samantha's family holds the same opinions as other ego-driven people. No one seeks a better life for it's just not possible. Beliefs of race consciousness cause them to sink further into limitation. Being unaware of affirmative principles, amid seas of negativity, greatly affects the way they think. No one, in Rebecca's opinion, is ready to change beliefs. [30]

Rebecca offers her amazed mother advice.

"Go for a walk," she implores. "You will not be any good to us if you're not good to yourself. Take some time, everyday, to sit outside, even if it's only for five minutes."

Samantha takes her advice and starts to walk short distances. She's finding life easier to deal with, as spirit instead of human. Business no longer matters.

Rebecca's health continues to decline. She goes from one emergency room to another when unbearable pain overwhelms her. Samantha spends much more time with Samuel. He seems to understand when she mistakenly refers to him as Daniel.

Samantha decides to write a book when the golden orbs stop appearing in July. It will be a book of her love for Daniel, about his life. She gathers memories to reassure her of their closeness throughout the years. The realization that Daniel prepared her for his passing, long before physical death, hits her like a ton of bricks. She believes a previous accident provided him with insight. Devastated with the thought, she's also profoundly grateful for this recognition.

Daniel was in the hospital five years before his last accident after hitting a pole while racing on a four-wheeler. The pole hit him directly in the heart and he remained unconscious for some time. She learned of the event when Rachel called her to come see him in the hospital days later.

Her spiritual self celebrates Daniel's graduation but she continues to grieve as a human. Sometimes, she tries to pretend that he's still physically alive. It's easy to believe his accident is only a grandiose way to escape from an unhappy life. A quick telephone call, and apology, from an exotic location, will alert her of his vitality and she'll be, oh, so happy to forgive him. They will rejoin, at an undisclosed place, to exist peacefully and happily, with everyone who means the most to them.

It's a comforting thought but, in the back of her mind, Samantha knows she can't lie to herself. Bargains, made long ago, must be kept. She again senses that Daniel and she planned their lives before birth into human form. And she understands that she must continue to live. It's a heart and gut-retching truth, for now it's her turn to live out the rest of a human life without Daniel.

Family gathers more than ever before. They again enjoy Ruth and Naomi's swimming pool after the Fourth of July. The weather is hot and humid. By this time, Samantha frequently surfs the Internet to learn more about spirit orbs. Data assures her that white spots in family videos and pictures note spirit activity. Orbs are more prominent in certain places, and especially visible, in pictures taken by the pool table. Daniel's aunts taught him how to shoot pool at an early age. They often gathered around the pool table as he played during family events.

Terrance and Momma ride home in Samantha's car when the party ends. Excitement fills the air as Terrance invites Samantha inside to see his new dog. Baby, a tiny Chihuahua with pointed ears, appeared one day when he opened the door. Harry is very happy to believe Daniel sent him Baby, just as he sent James the kittens.

Samantha feels compelled to take their picture. Two orbs are clearly visible as Terrance holds Baby, while standing near his son, Joel, and their brother Amos. Amos is now living with Terrance because he's again homeless. He swears, this time, he really is free of the crack habit that ruled his world.

Samantha remains hopelessly wrapped up in the drama of human life. The ego of race consciousness still consumes her. It will be more than three years before she finally realizes the Truth that her mind-body is an illusion. Sensing Daniel's presence later in August, she listens as words fill her mind. Daniel's soul directs her to remove books from the den bookshelf and relocate those important to her. She is not to look up at the den ceiling. Samantha places treasured books in Ziploc bags and stores them in the linen closet.

The roof on the back porch continues to leak even though roofers "repaired" it. Samantha knows it's going to be a busy season of storms in South Florida. She has no idea that Florida will take an unprecedented hit, feeling the brunt of four hurricanes and a tropical storm. Forecasters predict six to eight storms to become hurricanes during the 2004 Atlantic hurricane season. Two to four of them will develop into major hurricanes ranked as Category 3 or higher.

Appointments with Isaiah fall by the wayside as ego directs words and actions. Her gynecologist announces a new lump but the mammogram prescription remains hidden in a dresser. She vividly recalls Aunt Deborah's painful death after a series of operations and tests. Doctors completely removed one breast. But the cancer returned, even after bouts of radiation and chemotherapy. After they partially removed the other breast, she went through more radiation and chemotherapy. The memory of Aunt Deborah, taking Samantha's hand to place on her empty chest, still causes fearful thoughts.

"Don't ever let them do this to you," Aunt Deborah demanded forcefully grabbing Samantha's hand to move it over bony ribs.

Samantha decided right then and there that she didn't want breast cancer. If she got it, she would live joyously and not decrease her quality of life by wasting time and money on costly treatments.

Another doctor suggests a bone scan because of constant joint pain. Samantha is concerned over how the dye for the test will affect her already diseased bladder. She becomes severely depressed and begins to watch much more television.

Things no longer fall into place as easily as in the past. It is now much more difficult to do the work Samantha loves. She's losing faith in herself and feels her time is wasted. There seems little reason to continue after eight years of losses without meeting expenses or getting paid. Eight volunteers help to edit the newsletter but some now talk of ending their commitment.

In Samantha's mind, money is not an issue but James continues to push her to contribute financially to the household. Her role as community volunteer, commitment to household chores, cooking and banking, help further James' career, and watch Samuel means nothing. Fishing and work continue to be James' priorities as she fulfills family commitments.

Samantha decides to place the newsletter on the Internet to reduce costs. She hopes to meet a business goal of ten years by working two more years. Venturing out to a conference in New York, for people working in the field of hiv/aids, seems the perfect thing to do. She thanks God upon receiving a full scholarship. It's enough money for airfare, her hotel room, and the cost of the conference itself, which includes many meals. She soon decides that taking Rebecca along will be good for business. It seems like a good way to get away from increasing negativity.

Unhappy with life in general, Rebecca and Samantha decide to change their appearance. Rebecca buys blue contacts to wear with her now long, auburn hair. Samantha gets an extremely short haircut and dyes her hair to have brilliant auburn colored hair one last time. She's still ready to die. Her only option, she decides, is to be more spiritual than human.

Changing perception alters beliefs. Many things no longer concern her. Knowing that humans live to learn and teach lessons, helps her to realize that everything happens for a reason. In her gut, Samantha knows, family needs her a bit more to help them through more trials. She's determined to make the best of it and tries not to "sweat the small stuff." Samantha makes a new rule.

"Forget about it if it won't matter in three years."

James rarely talks about visits to see Abigail and Rachel. But after one visit, days before Rebecca and Samantha leave for New York, he surprises her with a short video of Abigail. Abigail wears a stuffed toy like a cape on her back. It consists of two, long, brown monkeys linked together like a backpack. The thought of someone with a "monkey on their back" enters Samantha's mind.

In the video, James asks Abigail to sing a song while she walks toward a bed. He expects her to jump up on the bed to sing about monkeys, too many monkeys jumping on the bed. She turns slowly and sings sweetly, as only a two-year-old can, "Twinkle, Twinkle, Little Star." Samantha knows Daniel's soul prompted her to sing the song, for it's one of their favorites. She sung it many times to both Daniel and then to Abigail as she rocked her to sleep. Daniel's soul is letting Samantha know, once again, he's still around and doing his best to guide those loved on earth.

Electronics are now a strong source of communication. Samantha likes to use the new refrigerator's ice cube dispenser while James prefers crushed ice. The small difference in preferences often causes a shouting match. One night the refrigerator stops dispensing ice cubes. The setting sticks on the crushed ice dispenser. Samantha senses Daniel's soul made the change, for James, to limit fights. It doesn't seem like much of a chore to reach into the ice bin for ice cubes.

Daniel's soul accompanies her more now than when in physical form. Songs on the portable CD player continue to change frequently as she drives. Daniel's voice fills her brain when she recognizes his presence. Samantha announces, it's funny, weird, that he can still make her heart feel full, even though he's dead. Yet, she's beginning to feel more as if she's crazy when listening to everyone else's opinion.

Daniel's soul stops coming to get her to be with

Abigail in the wee hours of the morning. It upsets her so she starts to imagine going there herself. After just a few mind trips, he tells her to stop. If Samantha continues to visit Abigail with her mind, it might harm her precious granddaughter. Since two family members are schizophrenics, Samantha thinks, people might think Abigail is too if she tells others about the visits. It seems possible that along with talk of Daddy's visits, which she already speaks of, people will think she needs "help." They might do something to harm her mentally. Samantha decides to stop frequent visits, in mind, to Abigail. (31)

30. Most humans are unaware of beliefs held by souls, including opinions from past lives. It's up to us to be aware of our ability to evolve once we're in human form.

The environment we're born into plays a role in our belief system. Before birth on earth, we choose the type of environment to live in based on how we need to grow as souls. As humans, we base conscious opinions on many things. Our environment includes what we learn from caregivers, and role models, especially from birth to six-years-old. Peer groups and other people can affect our beliefs as well. People can help us grow spiritually or harm us by taking our sense of self and power away to feed themselves. As Dr. Page notes, persistent and aggressive lost souls, in current lives, can smother the beliefs of others. Unaware of the true nature of humans, these souls disregard the truth others speak because they feel inferior. Awareness of the world can greatly change belief systems. Opinions change based on how we spend our time, what we choose to do, and where we choose to go.

Fearful people tend to limit themselves by always making excuses as to why they can't do something different or go somewhere new. Keeping an open mind and considering new information helps us to grow. Although it's hard to move from one's comfort zone, it helps immensely, to open the mind to greater possibilities. Attending classes or reading spiritual materials opens the mind much more than reading romance novels or watching television. Sadly, some people may not have access to new things as easily as others do.

Many people believe that we travel in spirit/soul groups throughout eternity. There's always a spirit from our group nearby to guide and protect us. There are both sincere spirit/soul groups who "live in the light" and insincere spirit/soul groups comprised of lost souls in need of love and help to evolve. It's important to only communicate with sincere, astute souls for they are aware of our Oneness.

Our species depends on how well we care for one another. Humanity's goals are to love and cherish all living beings, be in harmony with one another, and live in peace without the aggressive, fearful, and destructive threat of war. We can help each other by realizing the true nature of our being. We are all Good, we are all Light, and most importantly, we are all Divine Love, a part of our Creator.

31. Years later while reading Emmanuel's first book, Samantha's perspective on so-called insanity changes drastically. She is pleased to read, insanity is a healing, a wise soul decision, and people are spiritually in control. Many humans appearing insane may have experienced circumstances or trauma that they were not equipped to cope with. The decision of insanity helps them to learn while they contribute to the learning experience of others.

The words resonate as she thinks about family members who experienced traumatic events. She lived through a very rough year after her second divorce, while adjusting to life alone with two children. Instead of committing herself to an institution, she sent the children to Ruth and Naomi's while she toughed it out in private counseling.

:-)

~ 16 ~
Confirmation at Last

Issues continue to surface as James and Samantha's relationship deteriorates. Money seems like a big problem but she thinks they have more than needed. James is increasingly unhappy with his $60,000 a year job. Helping Daniel with unfinished business remains Samantha's top priority. She now spends more time with family and thinks Isaiah may find ways for her to help them. After hearing of her issues, and the instability of her marriage, Isaiah agrees to reduce his fee.

Confirmation that Daniel is indeed communicating comes when Samantha finally meets with Isaiah on August 8, 2004, four months and four days after Daniel transition. Isaiah's wife, Priscilla, sits in on the first session, for a short time, to verify several things. Samantha is missing many memories from the first ten years of life. Post-traumatic stress syndrome, from abuse during youth and throughout life, still affects her.

Isaiah knows Samantha can channel. He promises to help her break through more clearly to the Otherside when Priscilla leaves the room. They talk of reading auras, which is something new to Samantha. Learning how to read them is on his list of things to teach her. Samantha just wants to communicate with Daniel's soul.

Isaiah sits with eyes closed as Samantha watches. Minutes pass before he looks up with a smile to announce, slowly, three succinct words from the

Otherside.

"Don't bug me."

Samantha sits stunned for she watched part of a family video before seeing Isaiah. Daniel held up a Christmas present given to him from Naomi in the video. She crocheted a ladybug, and the words "Don't bug me," on a fly swatter. In the video Daniel held it up, wagged it back and forth, as if to slap at a fly, smiled, and said, "Don't bug me."

Doubts about Isaiah's ability to bring through information from the Otherside dissipate. Daniel, he says, is having a ball and doesn't want to be back in human form until he absolutely has to. Daniel wants Samantha to have fun too. It's a big request because she's still a workaholic. She now asks about Abigail. All she can do, Daniel relays, is send her white light and energy. Isaiah helps her learn how to do it. He then notes a young man standing to her right side. She fails to recognize the image described until a mental picture of her coworker, Luke, met in the early 1980's, comes.

"Yes," Isaiah agrees. "Luke is one of your spiritual guides. Luke," Isaiah notes with great interest, "is responsible, or as you feel, to blame, for getting you to start the hiv nutrition business." (32)

Samantha sits, shocked to the core. She worked many jobs but spent most time as a server. After moving to Florida, she worked as a baker, a luncheon server, and then a banquet waitress. Luke was a bartender she liked while working banquets at the Holiday Inn. One of the friendliest men she ever met, he became her first gay friend.

Luke always invited Daniel, Rebecca, and Samantha to his little rented house behind the property owner's big house. He lived less than a mile away so they got to enjoy the pool on hot summer days. Samantha loved being his taste-tester when he made new alcoholic drinks as they enjoyed many good times.

An automobile accident changed everything two years after they met. Luke lost control of his car, exiting from the highway in the wee hours of the morning, as he and his young lover, Mark, returned from the baths in Miami. The car overturned as he attempted the curve at a high rate of speed. Mark died from injuries related to the accident.

Police arrested Luke on the scene because he was drunk. He telephoned Samantha and several other friends days later. They agreed to keep some of his belongings until he got out of jail. Samantha stored several boxes in her garage. Luke was sentenced to prison for manslaughter several months later and began to write her.

Doctors diagnosed him with aids within his first year in jail. Samantha was dumbstruck. Along with concern for him was a concern for her children and herself. It was early in 1987 and she didn't have a clue as to how people got aids. She became a fanatic learning all she could about the disease.

Samantha never saw Luke again. He died within a year and she sent his things to his mother who lived in another state. By now, she had an associate's degree in Dietetic Technology and worked at a local hospital. Something told her that nutritional status was vital for people with aids. She felt drawn to hiv positive people like a moth to a flame.

Few people knew about aids and there was a great stigma attached to the word. Samantha was one of few nutritionists who saw aids patients as part of her job. She talked to them about food safety and good nutrition. Most of the hospital patients she saw were secretive about their positive hiv status. Visitors were required to take certain precautions when entering their room. Everyone had to wear a hospital gown, mask, and gloves. It made the patients feel isolated and very uncomfortable.

Samantha continued to help aids patients as she dealt with her own pain, extreme fatigue, nausea, bloating, and diarrhea. It became easier to help people as her health worsened because they experienced the same conditions. After two periods of physical therapy for neck and back conditions in late 1993, she had major surgery. It was the last of five abdominal surgeries. Her medical conditions worsened as she again started physical therapy for back pain. She began to have symptoms of an incurable disease after a series of respiratory and urinary tract infections. Years later, doctors diagnosed her with Interstitial Cystitis.

Many dietitians now asked Samantha for advice on how to treat aids patients nutritionally. Medical conditions forced her to think about working at home on her own terms. She volunteered at a local food bank for hiv-positive people. Doctors of food bank clients began to use her advice on nutrition as part of their patient care plans.

With the help of another volunteer, Samantha wrote her first nutritional services proposal for Ryan White funds. She treaded into unknown waters as the food banks first nutritionist when the government approved her grant application. Many people now considered her an expert in the field of hiv nutrition. Yet, she was not a dietitian for she had only a two-year degree instead of the four years required for dietitians.

Some food bank clients were patients met at local hospitals. Their doctors increasingly asked for dietary advice to help them. More local dietitians also asked for free dietary advice for their hiv-positive clients and patients as well. Everything seemed to be going well until politics reared its ugly head.

As hiv disease became more common, dietitians began to question why she didn't have a dietitian boss. They were not pleased that she was making a living using her expertise. There were no complaints about her free dietary advice but some of them felt they should do the nutritional counseling.

Her health continued to get worse and by the time the grant job ended, she decided to build a small business. Unfortunately, a new Florida licensure law passed concerning nutritionists. Registered Dietitian's (RD's) were protected by licensure but Dietetic Technicians who were registered (DTR's) were not. Samantha spent some time dwelling on the effort put into her hiv nutrition business. She didn't think she got the professional support that she deserved.

No one told Samantha about the possibility of being "grandfathered" into the new law. Legal precedent disallowed her as a nutrition consultant in Florida without supervision. DTR's could make a living only under the supervision of RD's or a variety of health care professionals "grandfathered" into the law. The list of those people included eye doctors, masseuses, chiropractors, medical doctors, and others. DTR's could work for non-profit companies or freely give away their services. They could not otherwise work on their own to make a living. [33]

Samantha began to concentrate on educating dietitians by designing a newsletter about nutrition and hiv. It was an intensive project and she had no idea where the energy came from. Still unable to pay herself, she thanked God that James financially supported them. Her lack of income soon caused serious disputes. But she remained committed to helping those with hiv. Samantha felt driven to increase the quality of life for people with hiv, even when James threatened to divorce her.

There were many times when she worked more hours than she thought she could. New thoughts occurred as she climbed into bed. Samantha would get up to follow the ideas and work several more hours. Whatever she needed to keep the business going would come whenever she thought the business totally bankrupt. Strangers asked to write articles or become editors. Some offered to help in different areas.

Now, because of Isaiah, she knows. Luke is the reason for it all. It makes sense as Isaiah speaks. Yes, Luke planted the thought of starting her business! She laughs and thanks Isaiah as he notes two other people named Luke needing recognition. Their identities remain a mystery until she recalls James's nephew Luke.

Isaiah verifies that she's to give him a message. Daniel wants Luke to know he's sorry for not spending more time with him. Disillusioned Luke recently returned home from college after the death of his roommate from a drug overdose. Samantha is to let him know that if he stays living at home, for now, everything will come together for him in the future. He will get the freedom he wants and so richly deserves.

Samantha promises to relay the message but the session ends before she learns the identification of the third Luke. Weeks later, a thought enters her mind. The funeral guest book, copied while at Rachel's house, holds one Luke. It turns out to be a coworker of Daniel's but is a dead end. She feels strongly that the third Luke has something for her, perhaps a message or something from Daniel. But the urgency to contact him lessens the next year. [34]

Isaiah and Samantha meet several times before he takes her through a past life regression. By then it's 2005 and Isaiah now sees Samantha without cost. *Through Time Into Healing*, by Dr. Brian Weiss, enthralls her. Based on the instructions within it, she investigates more past lives. Yet, she's surprised when Isaiah asks for permission to go back to a past life where they lived at the same time. She readily recognizes the past life as one recalled on her own months before. This time, she's able to recall more of the life.

Samantha sees mental images of this self very clearly. She's a young, black, slave girl riding in the back of a carriage through a field of wheat. Her body looks very thin and she's about 10-years of age. The girl's master is very big and stern looking. He drives the horse and buggy as his stone-faced wife sits beside him. Both he and his wife are dressed in black. The man has a white collar and a big, black hat like a pilgrim. Isaiah and Samantha continue to share details of what they see but then Isaiah begins to describe things Samantha doesn't see. He asks if she sees anything else. The regression ends when she becomes uncomfortable and fails to see more of the scene. A visibly upset Samantha then tells Isaiah that she senses her task is to end lives of bondage. She senses a thread of sexual, physical, and/or mental abuse throughout all her souls' lives.

Isaiah looks at her compassionately, hugs her like a father, and verifies that she no longer needs to live in limitation. Samantha, he relays as they walk to her car, is much more than she thinks. Without knowing why, she announces that if he abused her in the past, she forgives him. Isaiah thanks her. She promises to phone him for another appointment after time to think about their visit.

Isaiah and Priscilla move to northern Florida two weeks later. The move stuns Samantha but she senses they travel for a reason. The whole situation seems preordained. "Maybe their mission," she ponders, "is to search for certain people and I'm one of them."

Samantha's mind now opens further as she tries to communicate with her dad's soul. Sherman's soul soon drops by to let her know all is well. A strong urge, to take a break from work in the bedroom office, overwhelms her one day. Rising from her gray tweed computer chair, she walks into the living room to find the television on. She hasn't turned it on and now pushes the power button off.

The television refuses to turn off. There's no sound as she sits down stunned to watch the show. People run wild in streets that look familiar. Many of them start fires by throwing bottles of gasoline lit with matches. Cars are on fire, up and down the street, as people run amuck smashing storefront windows. Samantha picks up the remote control and tries to turn the television off again. It again refuses to turn off.

The television, she realizes with a start, is muted so she presses the mute button to turn the sound back on. As she tries again to turn the television off, she realizes the program is about the Detroit riots in the late 1960's. This time it turns off but comes back on when she starts to walk away. Sherman's clearly recognizable presence fills the room to stun her. She then realizes his energy turned the television on to get her attention.

Samantha was seventeen-years-old, while Daniel's father Peter was twenty-one and jobless, during the riots of Detroit. Peter hung out with a motorcycle club as Ruth and her friend Matilda helped Samantha care for Daniel. Sherman surprised them the morning after Detroit Police put them under a curfew. He went to their house to make sure they were okay.

Sherman got the biggest surprise. Samantha's house was full of people from the motorcycle club, forced to spend the night when police enforced the curfew. There were people scattered throughout the house. Some slept on the floor; some hurriedly got up and pretended to play cards. Others stood talking as they drank beer.

Sherman, Samantha now senses, dropped by to let her know he's okay on the Otherside. She thanks him for coming, tells him she loves him, and again turns the television off. This time it stays off and she doesn't feel her father's presence. "Yes," she thinks resolutely while smiling broadly, "I can sense and channel on my own."

32. Samantha learns years later that we all have many types of spirit guides who are always with us. It's simply a matter of being receptive to guides. Spirit communications occur in many different ways. Yet, one must avoid anything that does not resonate. Meditation, prayer, and opening our heart are the best ways to reach spirit guides. These guides speak to us when we are inspired or during sleep. Some guides are with us throughout our lives while others may suddenly appear to take care of a need and then disappear.

Personal Guides, entities known in previous lives, between lifetimes or even in our current lifetime, share a special affinity with us. They help by impressing our minds in subtle ways. Yet, these guides do not interfere with lessons or challenges that we chose to learn and grow from. Samantha sensed Daniel's role as that of a Personal Guide.

Luke fit the category of Mastery or Specialized Guide for he was the one that led her involvement in hiv, the virus that causes aids on earth. Samantha remained open to Luke's guidance while starting, and continuing, a financially unstable business.

Diseases such as aids and cancer force us to learn lessons of compassion, tolerance, understanding, and acceptance. Some people note this helps to balance negative karma created by our way of thinking about and behaving toward each other.

33. It's easy for Samantha to get into the drama of being a victim, once again. The drama helps her complete another part of her mission on earth. Many years later, as a student of <u>A Course in Miracles,</u> she recognizes lessons learned. The world's effort to separate humans into divisions is just another ego trick to keep them from knowing that earth is a dream world.

Samantha learns that everyone is a part of God. Each one is unique and has different gifts to offer the world. Yet, no one is separate from another. We are all part of God. Samantha forgives herself and the world for thoughts of separation. She then asks for forgiveness for even thinking she's in a real world and not a dream.

34. Samantha undoubtedly identifies the third Luke eight years later. Synchronicity guides her safely to one of his cabins in the woods of North Carolina to continue Lightworker tasks while the world continues to change drastically.

:-)

~ 17 ~
Revelations

Rebecca and Samantha leave for New York with thoughts of Daniel for he wanted to come along. The trio shared many trips and the prospect of Manhattan excited him. Samantha senses his essence will be there. She isn't disappointed. A variety of things, besides sporadic static and colored lights on videos, reveals his presence.

Both Tropical Storm Bonnie and Hurricane Charley head towards Florida but Samantha knows all is well. She's happy the usual pain in her left hip, which comes before hurricanes, fails to emerge. Her excitement never wavers, even when the pilot reroutes their airplane over deeper waters due to stormy weather. A late arrival proves useful while checking in at the hotel at 2:30 AM. The friendly, desk clerk awards  them a great room, on a higher floor, with a view of Broadway. It's the first of many, wonderful, hotel room views Samantha enjoys over the years.

Samantha's secret Nana Cam videos their first New York adventure while strolling through Central Park later in the morning. A unique blend of humanity offers many opportunities, to giggle with delight, as the camera hides inside a small tote bag, featuring a hole for the lens to stick out. Blue and fuscia-colored lights, spotted during playback, appear different from anything seen before. Diamond shaped lights move with the sun's reflection. They don't appear to result from a dirty lens for the camera was thoroughly cleaned before the trip.

Later, round lights appear in line with city's lights as they tour on a red, double-decked bus. Samantha associates some of them with spirit activity. Both Rebecca and Samantha feel Daniel's presence, especially when remarking on the architecture of New York buildings. Many years of working in the construction field graced him with a great appreciation for well-built structures. Images of Daniel, playfully moving his head in a circle, as he did when alive, fill her mind. He tauntingly repeats, "I'm in New York, I'm in New York."

Mindless chatter, singing out loud, and constant concerns over unimportant things consume her. But Daniel's presence is so strong that she senses it even with the constant mind activity. A sense of something bigger than themselves overpowers the women while at Ground Zero days later. Rubble of September 11, 2001 still lies beyond the gates surrounding the site. Drama heightens as the crowd views pictures posted of that fated day. "The Heroes of September 11, 2001" list is long. Samantha wonders why they haven't named them victims.

Feelings of tragedy and sadness surround them. The area suits her state of mind about the government. Building signs such as "Dissent is Patriotic," "No More Lies," and "No More War" fit beliefs. A middle-aged woman walks back and forth in front of the crowd. "Bush and the CIA attacked America on September 11th," she yells repeatedly, using her hands like a microphone.

Samantha senses much, more, destructive change for humanity in coming years. She doesn't want to be a part of it and has no idea how her view of the 9-11 event will change three years later after reading *A Course in Miracles* and *The Disappearance of the Universe*. [35]

Tropical Storm Bonnie makes landfall at 45 miles per hour south of Apalachicola, Florida while Rebecca and Samantha attend conference meetings. Bonnie's rainfall causes flooding and minor damage that worsens the next day.

Category 4 Hurricane Charley moves through Florida on August 13 and hits Punta Gorda harder than any other area. Their family remains safe.

Pictures Rebecca and Samantha take verify, at least for Samantha, that spirits are nearby. Both women feel Daniel's presence strongly at a cocktail reception on the evening that Hurricane Charley moves through Florida. It's the first time they relish in the experience of a New York nightclub.

As in the Keys, Daniel helps Samantha to enjoy herself. She's amazed to drink heavily and joyfully dance, after many years of inactivity, despite multiple medical conditions. Usually, her face flushes red, with increased blood pressure, despite medication. She often feels short of breath during exercise and her joints ache. Yet, a sudden surge of energy graces her when thoughts of collapsing on the dance floor arise.

Daniel's essence helps both women to stay safe and have a good time. When a man, from the conference, offers to escort them back to the hotel, Samantha knows it's Daniel's thoughtfulness. After stumbling down several streets, they crawl into separate beds and quickly pass out.

Both women scream and promptly sit up at 4:00 AM. Samantha, shaking, looks at Rebecca to ask if she had a nightmare. Rebecca quickly answers shaking her small, heart-shaped face to and fro, as if to remove the images.

"Yes, and it wasn't very pretty."

Shock fills them upon relating the same dream. The image of Daniel in a wheelchair, as a quadriplegic, like Christopher Reeve, haunts them. Rachel stands behind his wheelchair smiling. Abigail is at his left side with her right hand holding his.

In the dream, Daniel tells them he had a choice after the accident. He chose to leave his physical body. The revelation upsets them greatly as they cry together.

Samantha suddenly recalls reading about dreams that

people share of loved ones on the Otherside. Yet, she never imagined it would happen to Rebecca and her, even though they seem more in touch with his soul. They sense there's a choice to make. Do they choose to stay open to such communications or close themselves off? Rebecca chooses the later.

"I can't take it anymore Mom," she says with determination wiping tears away. "I have to go back to how I was."

Samantha understands but insists, "I'll never close my mind again. I've seen and experienced too much and know there's something much more to life than anyone believes."

Rebecca and Samantha stroll down Broadway on Sunday morning before leaving New York. Hordes of people from different cultures fill the streets. It's very exciting as they try to determine their origins. One man, dressed in a white shirt with tan slacks, stands on a street corner in the rain, straining his voice to yell loudly.

"Yahweh, Yahweh, Yahweh. I AM you. I AM you. I AM you."

They stop and listen for several minutes.

"Thank you, Thank you. Yahweh, Yahweh," he calls out raising his arms to the sky.

"Do you know what he's saying?" Samantha asks Rebecca. "Yahweh is another word for God. He's praising God."

Samantha truly understands his words next year. [36]

Samantha's beliefs continue to change upon returning from New York as she starts a book for Abigail. It's now vital for her granddaughter to know what kind of person her dad was. Friends and family try to get her out of the house but the book consumes her.

Samantha relents to attend one-year-old PJ's birthday party on a Sunday afternoon at the Rainforest Café. She thinks it's an expensive place to eat and wants to see it. PJ's father is one of James' employees. The family shared dinners, Keys vacations, and other times. Daniel's loss affects his parents more strongly now that they have their own son.

Today Samantha spends most of her time making a video of the party for PJ's parents. It's easy to do and makes her feel good. Near the events end, she holds back tears as PJ's parents joyfully scoop him up for a group hug amid many gifts. She thinks about how differently she raised Daniel. His words enter her mind as tears begin to fall.

"It's okay Mom," he says consoling her. "You did what you could." (37)

Joy increases later when she plays back the video to hear static alerting her to Daniel's presence.

Mary is the next person to distract Samantha with a free ticket to see the Dalai Lama in the future. Samantha is anxious to hear what he has to say about turmoil in America.

Many people think the last two elections were rigged. Polls turned thousands of people, eligible to vote, away before casting ballots. Computer votes changed. Workers found many untallied ballots after Republican Katherine Harris made the final decision. Most Floridians voted for Kerry and Edwards but Harris secured the presidency for George W. Bush. Samantha tried to get around the corruption of the first election by mailing her absentee vote for the second election. Yet, thousands of absentee ballots were "lost." Voting, she now decides, is a waste of time and effort.

Government intrusion seems to increase with each change to the familiar system. Samantha feels that the only real news is on CSPAN and some of the foreign television channels, available only through satellite dishes. Two companies now own 78% of the media. She senses it's going to get worse. Samantha believes that cable television severely limits what people see. The thought fills her with dread and fear.

She's fearful of other things as well. Amos remains in jail for assaulting Terrance. He succumbed to the urge for crack after living with their younger brother for several months. It's again hard to see him but at least they know he's safe.

Weather patterns concern her. More hurricanes are forming and she feels guided to put family videos onto DVD's. She believes it's because they'll be easier to store and transport. It seems like a good idea since DVD players are becoming more common than VCR players are. Years later, she'll use the DVD's to write her first three books accurately.

Transferring family VCR's onto DVD's is a huge project. It takes lots of time and effort and she has to buy special equipment to do it. She easily finds needed equipment and the project rewards her more than anything accomplished since Daniel's transition does. It frees her mind from grief and fear of the future. She becomes more open to Daniel's communications because she isn't as consumed with his loss.

Daniel's soul guides her daily. While watching family videos, she sees how he helped his family through a gradual transition, by spending less and less time with them during the two years before physical death. Samantha still misses him terribly but knows his soul continues to help loved ones. Joel, his cousin who dreams of a career in wrestling, confides that he too feels Daniel's presence. Samantha fondly recalls many wrestling matches her grandpa took her to see at Cobo Hall in Detroit.

Ruth's birthday, in late August, offers a work break as several family members meet at a local restaurant for dinner. Samantha senses Daniel but remains silent. The family still believes she sees and senses things that are not there. She's tired of their teasing ways and knows it's hard to believe in things if you don't have first-hand experience. Closed minds, she often feels, detrimentally affects soul's growth.

Five, of eighteen, celebration pictures hold spirit energy so Samantha shows them to her family. No one believes the white spots are spirit orbs.

    Ruth and Naomi's birthdays are less than a week apart. They decide to celebrate them with a family party at their house several days before Ruth's hernia surgery. Ruth is scared and depressed. Hernias, it seems, are part of family history, for Sherman, Daniel, and Samantha experienced the same surgery. Samantha will soon learn to disbelieve thoughts about family genes as her spiritual education progresses. (38)

    Following Daniel's instructions, Samantha brings part of a family video for Ruth to see. His presence fills the air as she pops it into the video player. The video is of Daniel during a family vacation. He stands before the camera with a smile on his face and a joint in his mouth.

    "You're going to have to edit this video," he teases Samantha, getting ready to light the joint.

    "I don't edit my videos," she says. "When I die you'll be the one to see it, not me."

    "Die, die, die, that's all you talk about, is dying. What you need is an attitude adjustment."

    Daniel jeers, pretending to be a boxer punching his fists towards her, before speaking joyfully.

    "Life is good. The world is good. Enjoy yourself."

    No one in the family is ready to see Daniel's face. They all reprimand Samantha for showing Ruth the video. No one believes it's Daniel's way of telling Ruth not to worry.

    Samantha's camera always captures at least one spirit orb during family gatherings. A pinkish orb appears in the new party video. Several digital pictures also hold orbs. The family remains skeptical. They secretly talk of getting her committed to an institution for the mentally unstable.

    Floridians focus, once again, on Hurricane preparations in early September. Samantha videos her home office as the clock strikes midnight. She thinks having a video of business equipment will be a good idea if the storm is bad. An orb, accompanied by static, delights her. The familiar noise nearly drowns out equipment descriptions and values.

The next evening she videotapes kittens on the back porch. A small orb passes in front of the camera and slowly moves through the glass door. Samantha replays the videotape at half speed, several times, to confirm the event. She decides not to show it to anyone.

Nearly three million Floridians leave their homes before Hurricane Frances hits. She makes landfall on Hutchinson Island, as a Category 4 hurricane, in the early hours of September 5. Rachel's house sits in an area more affected by the storm. She and Abigail spend two days on the floor of her home office, which fortunately sits next to the third bathroom. Several trees uproot and shingles tear from the roof as the storm rages on.

Fifteen people die as Frances batters Florida for more than thirty hours. But her wrath spares the area near most family. As many others, they're left without electricity but consider it a minor thing. Samantha knows Daniel's essence protects Rachel and Abigail as James leaves to help clear storm debris.

Daniel's soul urges Samantha to shut down the desktop computer and printer to store safely away. The computer system became her life, upon feeling the full brunt of empty nest syndrome, when Rebecca left home in May of 1991, so it's difficult to do. She keeps business equipment on constantly while communicating with people from all over the world. Having Daniel's special Mother's Day gift on her desktop computer makes it even more precious to her.

Samantha resigns herself to working on the laptop, purchased earlier in the year, as older equipment sits stored in the closet. This effort is one of many making it easier for her to let go of worldly things.

Hurricane Ivan hits Alabama on September 16 and crosses over southern Florida on September 21, 2004.

Samantha sees the Dalai Lama with Mary two days before the storm hits Florida. The audience sits spellbound by the Dalai's sense of humor and boyish charm. His message moves them deeply and Samantha is happy to be there. She suddenly feels Daniel's presence.

"Samuel was born to help you get over the loss of me," he announces softly.

The truth of Daniel's words sting like a slap in the face. Memories flood awareness as she begins to cry. Guilt overwhelms her.

Rebecca played in the South Florida Junior Philharmonic Orchestra, conducted by James Judd, while in high school. But she dropped out of school before graduation just as Samantha had. When Rebecca became pregnant at 18-years-old, Samantha had no idea what a pivotal role Samuel would have in her life. She didn't want Rebecca to have the child but thought her daughter would come back home, finish high school, and play the violin.

Now Samantha spends much more time taking care of Samuel. Watching him is one of the few things that make her feel happy.

More than one million homes and businesses lose power in several states, including Florida, when Hurricane Ivan hits. Ivan is blamed for twenty-five deaths in the U.S. Eight of them are in the Florida Panhandle. The eastern edge of the storm leads to tornadoes before the eye hits. Like Frances, this storm's force is closer to Rachel's house. James again helps Rachel after the storm.

James is now Samantha's only physical link to Abigail and Rachel. She begins to think that perhaps she's meant to lose him. Maybe he's supposed to be with Rachel and act as Abigail's new dad. The thought comforts her for she's still hoping to die. Most of Samantha's family talks of the closeness between James and Rachel. She knows no one will be surprised if they end up together.

Changing consciousness continues to wreck havoc

with the world. On September 25, Hutchinson Island is targeted for a second time, as Category 3 Jeanne hits after devastating Haiti. Hurricane Jeanne makes landfall two miles from where Frances struck (http://en.wikipedia.org/wiki/2004_Atlantic_hurricane_season).

Hurricane rains cause more damage to the leaking roof at James and Samantha's house. The den ceiling cracks and begins to leak near the bookcase. As rain seeps through the wood, the back porch ceiling begins to break apart again. James puts coolers on the floor to catch the rain as it seeps through the roof. Samantha ignores it all to watch the movie of Samuel and herself clearing out a closet. She again notices static on the videotape.

Constant criticism seems to surround Samantha when near James. What little communication developed in the past is gone. Her connection to the Otherside through Daniel consoles her. She's glad his soul warned her to be ready for bad weather. The season turns out to be well above average in activity with fifteen named storms. Experts cannot fully explain the shift in hurricane activity to more hurricanes, and storms that are more powerful.

Daniel asks Samantha to stop working on the book about him when she gets to the last Christmas they should have spent together. Still feeling it too difficult to be human, she enjoys her connection to the Otherside and longs to be there. She doesn't want to be a human again. Thoughts now dwell on staying between realms to be a teacher for humans after physical death.

35. The Disappearance of the Universe reminds us, we all agreed to be on earth during these trying times. Souls consciously agree to be part of tragedies to help other souls. Everyone came with an unconscious knowledge of what was going to happen. The trick is that we have to remember who we truly are. Events such as September 11 are wake-up calls, undeniable symbols to help us remember that we created this dream world. We have never, nor will we ever, be apart from

God.

36. *The light of God is in us. We exist in a Universal God soup connected to all living things. We are, in essence, parts of the Divine Being. I AM, that, of which I AM!*

37. *Daniel's soul made a contract with Samantha's soul before birth to assure the best possible growth. Samantha gave Daniel's soul the experiences needed to evolve.*

38. *A mental attitude keeps people locked into believing they must suffer through illness. Holmes notes the subconscious mind is "the builder of the body" and the subjective mind creates what we think. Subconscious suggestions become memories that externalize in the body unless we change the way we think. If we believe that a certain illness "runs" in the family, our body makes it so. Conscious thought can erase memories and heal disease.*

:-)

~ 18 ~
The Burden Increases

Samantha feels Daniel slowly pulling away as she becomes more able to cope with his loss. Earth, intuition reveals, is a place to learn, to teach one another, to come to love and feel what it's like to be human. It was Daniel's destiny to die when, and as, he did. He graduated upon learning lessons and fulfilling goals.

Daniel's soul now chooses inspiring songs for her to hear while listening to the memorial CD. The CD player skips over songs to play "Soak up the Sun," by Atlantis Morissette, whenever she's sad, or depressed. No one is to blame for his physical death. Daniel's soul made sure the song went on the CD because it's about enjoying oneself and not blaming anyone for anything.

Being human, Samantha continues to believe, is a burden. She senses worsening world situations and doesn't want to live much longer. There will only be more weather trials, more illness, and more problems. Daniel will always be near, as promised, just not in the expected way.

Dr. Page, author of *Spiritual Alchemy*, verifies beliefs years later as avid reader Samantha smiles broadly. Veils between dimensions continue to thin and those of the spirit world, who love and support us, meet us in dreams, and meditations, to offer encouragement and guidance.

Daniel's soul continues to guide as Samantha gains more insight into the unknown. Insight rarely appears in dreams, for she always wakes crying, filled with grief. Her loss is devastating, in human terms, and she doesn't think she will ever recover. Daniel's soul finds much better ways to communicate by using the music they love. He speaks as she tries to study or work. But now, she wonders what "level" he's on, or if he has the information needed, to guide her.

James quits his job in October and Samantha's Shangri-la becomes increasingly negative. Daniel's soul continues to try and cheer her up. She filled the house with sadness, and grief, and now it's time to clear it away. It's time to raise the energy to insure that when his soul transitions, she'll be able to function, seemingly alone.

Family members stop listening so she branches out to anyone who will. Passing on information, Samantha makes suggestions as to what part of the country to live in. She advises people to stay away from areas with faults (making it more likely for earthquakes) or military bases where the chance of attack might be greater.

Samantha feels the need to help the world towards reaching its goal. She isn't sure what that goal is but tells friends that humans are meant to learn lessons and be reborn, many times. Everyone, she senses, must love each other and strive for world peace.

In late October, Ruth and Samantha take Momma to visit their sister Sarah, who lives four hours away. Pink colored diamond shapes from the sun's reflection catch Samantha's eye for the first time. Although Hurricane Ivan turned at the last minute, to spare their neighborhoods, other areas show widespread damage. Ruth counts fourteen dead turtles along the roadway as Samantha videotapes the destructive path of the hurricanes. Many road signs are missing or damaged and it's sad to think of people getting lost without signs to direct them. They soon joke about the missing roof tiles of a rented weekend villa. Daniel's essence laughs with them for static

blocks the sound of laughter from the video.

The next morning they motor down I-4, near Orlando, to get Sarah. A lone bird flies next to the van as Samantha sings loudly to "Soak up the Sun." She knows Daniel wants everyone to understand the message.

Days after their trip, family enjoys Ruth and Naomi's boat. It's Ruth and Naomi's thirty-fourth year together as James tries to help, by taking Daniel's place as boat captain. Samantha still feverishly transfers family videos onto DVDs so she's happy for the break. When Samuel voices displeasure as Samantha videos, Rebecca reminds him that memories are all they have of Daniel.

Samuel and Samantha yell their hellos to Amos as the boat passes the county jail. Of course, Amos can't hear them. Samuel tells him to say hello to Martha Stewart and the family roars with laughter. Samantha feels Daniel directing her to say certain things during the four-hour boat ride. She tries to entertain everyone but it just annoys them all.

Upon their return, James moves out of the boat, to get the van to back onto the ramp. Ruth leans over, just a bit, and starts to get onto the dock. Suddenly, it looks as if someone shoves her. Her butt jerks forward as if pushed by unseen hands. Her knees buckle and she falls with a loud splash into the water. They all roar with laughter knowing Daniel's essence played a role in the mishap. Ruth stands in the murky water looking like a drowned rat.

Life becomes more difficult in November when James' unemployment benefits equal merely a third of usual pay. Samantha remains thankful James spends one day each week with Rachel and Abigail. It offers her time alone and a way to keep in touch with them. She also feels fortunate to spend more time with Samuel.

Everything seems to change much more quickly. Medical conditions require more time, and although she's lost sixteen pounds since Daniel's death, Samantha is still obese. A pinched neck nerve further affects sleep. She plans days around medications, gastritis, food, fluids, and other body limitations, while waiting for Social Security to approve a disability claim filed last year.

Samantha and friends are now concerned more than ever by the loss of democracy. Traffic cameras (http://host.maptuit.com/fdot/?config=TrafficW.FDOT&aoi=0) are increasingly evident on many roads and places like public parks. Samantha wonders if they're hooked up to satellite dishes like those in New York.

Each day she sits in front of the television to tape hours of CSPAN, which shows live Senate and House hearings. She plans to save the tapes for her grandchildren. No one with political clout talks about the elections. Samantha suspects it's to keep the stock market up and limit riots. So where is the underground movement to take back democracy? She wonders. How can Americans teach democracy, to other countries, when they don't have it themselves? She's disgusted to be an American, especially one in Florida.

Rebecca and Samantha still feel the loss of Daniel immensely. They're thankful that James now spends more time with Samuel. Rebecca's health is not much better than Samantha's is as she moves from one emergency room to another. She finally, as mom did years ago, agrees to another exploratory surgery. [39]

Samantha accepts things as they come. She hopes situations will improve but her faith in God is sorely lacking. Things are not coming as easily as before. People are not sending articles to publish in the business newsletter. Volunteers stop asking if she needs help. And the telephone line seems constantly busy with personal issues. It's almost as if an unseen force cuts the cord on her business. She decides to cut her workload. Feeling it's time to care for herself, she decreases newsletter publication from six times a year to four.

It's time to find a new way to good health and well-being. Each drug prescribed causes more limitations. Western medicine is failing Samantha so, after months of uncertainty, she makes an appointment to see one of her editors, Michael, a Doctor of Oriental and Naturopathic Medicine.

Her first treatment results are better than Western medicine has ever achieved. It's the first time, in more than a year, that she feels such relief. Both sinuses open, for the first time in years, allowing her to breathe deeply, and the swelling on her right side lessens. Her senses heighten and she feels an increased awareness of being while driving home. One treatment helps to free the pinched neck nerve and decreases body numbness as well.

Samantha's body doesn't tingle or feel numb during the night now. It's easier to walk for the first time in more than a year. Michael is just as happy as Samantha when she telephones days after treatment. He offers to continue helping even if she can't pay as much as other patients. She decides to continue the scraping and cupping treatments for his method works well.

39. Life situations change as our soul planned before birth. Everything happens for a reason. Illness is a wake-up call. It can occur when we don't listen to our soul and aren't growing spiritually. Body areas, Emmanuel notes, "that resist the soul consciousness can develop dysfunction depending on the needs of our soul."

If we allow them to, illnesses offer an opportunity to mentally, and emotionally, confront what we are reluctant to see. How we deal with situations and conditions matter. Changing our perspective may not be easy to do but can help greatly. It's much easier to change the way we think when we change lifestyle habits. Reading self-help books and watching less television makes a big difference.

:-)

~ 19 ~
Drama All Around

Terrance hosts the family's first Thanksgiving Day without Daniel. His wife and son moved on and he now refers to himself as Terry. Everyone acts on their best behavior while placing food on the table. Samantha sits in the living room as they eat. Medication schedules require her to wait two hours before eating.

A new energy seems to flow between James and Rachel when she arrives with Abigail later in the evening. They are all happy to see them. It's the first time since her wedding to Daniel that Samantha remembers seeing makeup on Rachel. "Perhaps," Samantha thinks, "she's trying hard to make someone jealous."

Abigail sits next to Papa James upon entering the house. They both wear red shirts as if in secret agreement. New, red, cowboy boots, worn earlier to ride a pony for the first time, accent Abigail's tiny feet. She excitedly tells unemployed Papa about the horse she wants for Christmas. Rachel acknowledges everyone with a hug, and a kiss, except James. They ignore one another for the first hour. It seems odd to Samantha because he still visits with Rachel and Abigail during the week.

Abigail clearly mesmerizes James as they sit together. He continuously moves her long hair from in front of her face. The loving gesture surprises Samantha immensely. She has never seen him act in such a loving way. James' love for Abigail looks much stronger than any love Samantha has seen him display.

Photos of them show unexplainable white lights. They first appear on James' torso and upper lip, but then a bright, white light appears on the bridge of his broad nose, along with three more on his closed right eye. Spirit orbs float in other pictures as well.

Samantha longs to hold Abigail but consoles herself with the thought that her Nana Cam captures the day. Everyone listens politely as Rachel announces holiday plans. A hush falls over the room as Rachel talks about celebrating Christmas holidays, out of town, with a male friend from high school. Rachel's friend now lives up north with his wealthy family. They own lots of land and look forward to seeing her and Abigail. Disappointment fills the room. It saddens Samantha to think they'll miss Abigail's third birthday for it falls on the day after Christmas.

Samuel's birthday is the next day. Samantha and Rebecca try not to think about the loss of his only strong role model. Daniel always made an effort to be there for Samuel. He knew what it was like to grow up without a father. The boy is older now and really needs that male connection. Papa James sometimes takes Samuel fishing but never seems to have a strong interest in his welfare.

Rebecca hosts a small, family, birthday party for Samuel's twelfth year. Two of his friends attend the celebration. The family remains outside on the back porch to enjoy the wonderful, late November weather. It's nearly 80 degrees and still too hot for Samantha. She videotapes, feeling Daniel's presence, moving from the porch to the air-conditioned house frequently to get away from the heat. Samuel and friends play video games in his bedroom while James watches television in the living room alone.

Everyone laments over Daniel while playing their usual pinochle card game. Samantha gets two double runs in a row.

"I'm not stacking the deck." She announces with a wink. "I can't help it if someone else is stacking the deck."

Rebecca, her partner, gets a double run in the next hand. As they play, a tiny, flash of light passes to the right side of Samantha's head. She leans towards Rebecca while singing along to a popular song on the radio.

"I've got to keep moving on."

"Yup, he had his fun," Rebecca replies.

"You realize that when Daniel died I lost my pinochle partner," Ruth reports sadly.

"We all lost a little piece of ourselves," Samantha notes. "But inside us all there's a little piece that helps us carry on."

They all know Samantha refers to the first song on Daniel's memorial CD.

"And that little piece sticks around and gives us three double runs in a row," Rebecca announces grinning widely.

"And then he goes and plays with his daughter," Samantha tells the group. "Right now, Abigail is pointing to his side of the bed going, Daddy's there. Don't put your hand there Mommy, Daddy's there."

"Yeah, did you hear Rachel saying that?" Rebecca asks Ruth.

"Yeah, she did," says Samantha. "She still sees him. Daniel's spirit will always be with Abigail."

Words from a song on the radio waft through the silence, "and you heal yourself away, and you heal yourself away. And you heal and you heal." Rebecca jumps up from her chair.

"I've heard enough," she shouts, silencing the radio.

"And he checks in on each and every one of us," Samantha adds winking.

Rebecca glares angrily toward her while standing near the CD player.

"What are you doing girlie?" Samantha asks taking a swig of her drink, a strong Myer's Rum and Coke.

"I was trying to put a CD in but it won't play."

"Maybe your bo, bo doesn't want to hear it. Put a different one in. It works for me."

The family stares at Samantha as if she's crazy.

Rebecca places a CD by Journey, one of Daniel's favorites, into the player. It's one of the CDs played repeatedly while driving from Michigan to Florida to begin their new life in 1982. The CD begins to play flawlessly.

"Is that the one you wanted to play?" Samantha asks.

"No," Rebecca replies sitting down in a huff to light another cigarette.

Samantha knows Rebecca intuitively put the CD in for her brother.

"Don't stop believing. Hold on to that feeling," she sings while pointing to Rebecca.

No one knows Samantha's full, thirty-two ounce container of diet soda holds four shots of rum. She's now feeling its effects.

Photos of the party show numerous spirit orbs. Samantha knows Daniel's spirit is among them. Daniel continues to tell her everything will turn out okay. He wants her to have fun. His words, said during their Keys vacation in 2001, ring through her brain.

"Life is good. The world is good. Enjoy yourself."

Life continues to alter rapidly but Samantha knows she's capable of withstanding change. She's changed her life so many times that it makes her head spin to think about it. Samantha is a survivor and has already lived numerous lives within her current one. A teenage marriage lasted little more than a year. Marriage to Rebecca's father took place after the couple lived together for four years. It ended in divorce three years later.

James and Samantha's marriage, unstable since 1992, continues to worsen. They now seriously question the relationship. Arguing reaches new heights one evening in the living room. As soon as James raises his voice, the television turns off to get their attention. It's a new television and there's no power outage. Samantha senses Daniel's spirit. The yelling match ends before it begins when she thanks him for being there. James puts his arm down, shakes his head in disbelief, and walks back to his den.

They both realize it's again time to calmly discuss the

relationship. Words to say fill Samantha's brain but she's not sure of their source. She follows James into the den to announce that his reality is not hers. They cherish very different priorities in life and very different beliefs.

James and Rachel, she confides, are meant to be together. He's to be a father to Abigail. There are no strong blood ties between James, Daniel, Rachel, Abigail, or anyone in the family, so she doesn't see it as a concern. Rachel and Abigail feel comfortable with him and look forward to his weekly visits. Samantha says it's okay if he and Rachel get together.

"You know," replies James with a steady stare, "Abigail really cares for and depends on me to tell her how Rebecca and Terry are doing."

Samantha never really felt James truly loved her and it's usually a struggle to communicate. Words now pour forth in a steady stream. She notes her priorities. They're not money, possessions, or power, but spiritual growth.

"There are at least," she notes calmly, "nine more years left for me to live and at least two of them will be spent on continuing to educate the world on hiv nutrition. You, on the other hand, appear unconcerned over war, loss of democracy, or the rape of spiritual growth, world peace, and universal love."

She relays that her friend, Luke, helped guide her into the business after physical death.

"You're crazy," James says as she continues to speak.

"There's more to a marriage than financial support," Samantha informs him. "Our marriage drains my human host and stops me from helping the children the way I want to. After carrying the burden of a variety of health conditions for more than ten years, I'm finally ready to return to my soul's true path. Sometimes," she remarks with a long sigh, "love isn't enough. Perhaps we'll go onto different paths and that's okay. I'll always love you and I'm willing to stay in this marriage. But if you decide on divorce, I'll agree."

"How will you care for yourself," he calmly inquires.
"Don't worry about how I'll live," she announces with a broad smile, not really knowing the answer. "Things will happen, as they should. Friends with similar beliefs will meet my needs as they arise."

Samantha has no idea why she says the words. Esther remains her only close friend and she still lives in Michigan.

An appointment with Michael, hours later, serves as a blessing. Michael talks of Chinese medicine, and spiritual things, making Samantha grateful to be in the presence of someone with similar beliefs. His scraping and cupping method works amazingly well to relieve body pains and it feels good to have someone to confide in. She feels, and sees, blood flowing more quickly through her hands and down her inner thighs as he works. The burning in her bowels lessens offering great, long overdue, relief. They talk for several minutes after the treatment. He tells her not to worry about the cost as they hug goodbye.

Feeling the dread of returning home, Samantha fights tears while walking toward the car. Joy fills her after pushing the CD player's on button. The player beeps several times, skips over songs, and just as she begins to sing, as in his human host, Daniel's spirit changes the song. Upon voicing her distress, the CD player glides through songs for several minutes. It's difficult to determine what song plays while sensing Daniel's strong presence. She places her right hand on the passenger seat and again hears everything will be all right.

Daniel's comforting presence stays until she reaches home thirty minutes later. Samantha hears only her two favorite songs play through and knows, without a doubt, that nothing else matters. We are who we truly are. It's a knowing. But she doesn't yet remember that we are spirits in human form.

Samantha makes James dinner and then eats in what she refers to as her bedroom, the front home office, trying to work. James eats in front of the television. A short while later, he switches channels to a show with Dr. Wayne Dyer. She remembers reading one of Dr. Dyer's books about pulling strings many years ago. He now discusses being our spiritual selves.

It's no coincidence that James listens to Dr. Dyer, for ten to fifteen minutes, before leaving the room and returning to change the channel.

"Free will," she thinks, "there's always free will."

Samantha offers blessings, and thanks, to the force within us all, Universal Consciousness. Having not yet learned that we are each unique parts of One, she asks the white light to surround the "chosen people" to help them find the path to their true destiny.

"My children," she thinks, "were not raised in secure, nurturing environments, especially not Daniel."

Now actions focus towards creating that perfect environment for her grandchildren. [40]

40. Samantha remains unaware that blessing people increases the frequency of guiding coincidences. She's achieved the Eighth Insight but doesn't know how to increase the effectiveness of thoughts. Daniel's spirit soon leads her to groups of people with heightened awareness to propel her further toward the mission of a Lightworker.

The author of <u>Celestine Prophecy</u>, James Redfield, notes it's extremely important for children to be among people who nurture their energy, to assure early security and growth.

:-)

- 171 -

~ 20 ~
Christmas Holiday Begins

Everyone in the family seems to experience life changes. Rebecca's scheduled surgery gives Samantha new incentive to improve physically. Michael's Eastern medicine treatments allow her the opportunity to begin lifting the burden of an arduous medication schedule. Still out of work, James asks Samantha, "What will it cost me to divorce you?"

She asks Ruth and Naomi to host the family's Christmas for it seems impossible to act as usual. Sometimes, she isn't sure why she does, or says, certain things but knows things happen for a reason. The reason always escapes her. Samantha only knows she's where she is supposed to be, doing what she is supposed to do, finally taking care of herself. Besides continuing her business, she offers support to help family with spiritual growth. Yet, no one seems to understand and sometimes Samantha doesn't either. Family caters to her, pretending to listen, but they all think, "She's crazy."

Both Rebecca and Samantha give up cell phones since the costs are beyond their means. Conducting business through the house phone becomes nearly impossible as James surfs the Internet or talks with fishing buddies. Samantha makes it a source of stress instead of recognizing it for what it is, another clue to let go of the business and move on to a greater cause.

Her case for disability remains undecided after seventeen months. Money is a constant worry. Last year, after more than twenty years, child support came from her two ex-husbands. Now it's time to use the money for more than just family vacations.

An avid angler, James continues to fish up to three times a week amid visits with Rachel and Abigail. Samantha remains thankful even though pictures of their times together are rarely shared. Knowing Abigail has fun when he visits is enough for her.

The atmosphere at home feels more negative with each passing day. James tries to fix the roof, which has leaked for almost a year, and closes the large gap in the back porch ceiling. But he ignores the hole in the den ceiling inside the house. That hole bothers Samantha much more. She fears that anything in the attic can come into the house so she keeps her office door closed and tries not to think about it. The home office becomes her sanctuary and she sleeps there often.

Samantha feels it will soon be her time to go Home. She lights candles before bedtime but doesn't know why. Sometimes she lights candles during the day and prays for God's deliverance. Health care is a constant worry without insurance. But now, visits to her regular doctor of many years are free. He gives her complimentary samples of many prescribed drugs. The two specialists, seen regularly, also discount the cost of services. And the one drug that relieves the fire in her bladder now comes in the mail, free through the company. The drug's cost is almost $400 a month so she's grateful to have the specialist arrange for delivery.

Samantha tries not to think about human issues and opts for the attitude that, "It is what it is." Now she spends more time alone. Several family members still sense Daniel's presence periodically. Most ignore the so-called "coincidences" but Samantha continues to pay attention. Daniel's spirit guides her to make friends with people who believe as she.

Samantha no longer fits into the family mold and feels very different from loved ones. She feels like the black sheep of the family because no one holds her new beliefs. The way she talks, along with the pictures she shows of spirit orbs, make them all feel uncomfortable. It reminds her of receiving her first community college degree. No one else in her family felt the desire to attend college then. They all told her she was too arrogant when she got her degree.

Still missing Daniel during family events, Samantha doesn't want to celebrate her fifty-fourth birthday. The last two birthdays ended in disappointment when everyone became negative. Last year, they celebrated at her favorite seafood restaurant but she felt empty when it was over. She decides to join family for dinner only because of Rebecca's repeated requests. Samantha hopes this year will be different. Maybe this year everyone will be in a good mood.

It's an odd birthday. Since family doesn't want to see her pictures, Samantha leaves the old camera at home. No one else brings one. It's time to stop noting the past but Samantha will not know that for years to come.

The dinner party starts badly before they enter the restaurant. Samantha doesn't mind the short wait outside for a table, during early bird hours, but other family members do. Naomi, known for being critical of just about everything, arrives later in a negative mood. She's usually the first one to criticize. Other people are wrong if they don't act like her. Family interactions often change from positive to negative as others share her opinions.

Samantha senses Naomi's moodiness when she joins the table and complains about the fancy restaurant. Complaints begin with a look at the silverware and continue about menu prices and choices. Customers at other tables look at her family with dislike in their eyes. Ever critical Naomi orders chicken while the rest of the family eats seafood. She continues to complain saying the service is either too slow or too attentive. Samantha doesn't know why Naomi continues to disrupt her birthday celebration until she starts to read *A Course in Miracles*. [41]

Everyone tries to ignore Naomi's frequent and loud complaints. But the more they try to be positive, to offset negative remarks, the more complaints they hear. Naomi's power play works well. She gets their energy as they give her attention. Naomi leaves the restaurant feeling strong when everyone else feels like they've been run over by a Mack truck.

Samantha doesn't know what's really happening until she learns about power games from the *Celestine Prophecy*. [17] The book details how earth life changes, as more people understand certain insights to life. Power games are ways that humans use to steal other peoples energy. Stealing someone's energy causes the victim to feel powerless and fearful. Everyone steals energy, by making people pay attention to them, either aggressively, or passively, by playing on people's sympathy or curiosity. The action usually takes place without either person knowing what's happening.

The night could have turned out differently with a change in perception. Everything becomes clearer as Samantha studies *A Course in Miracles* years later. By then, she knows Naomi, as a human, took everyone's energy. Learning why people take energy from others opens Samantha's mind to a whole new world. [42] As souls, Naomi and Samantha planned this, and many other events, to wake her up to the truth of their real identity. We are One, parts of God, powerful beyond belief.

A family trip to see Rachel, Abigail, and Joy, before they leave for the holidays, offers more insights to life. Christmas decorations fill the large house and grounds. A huge, decorated Christmas tree sits in the large living room. This is the first year that Samantha does not buy a tree, since leaving home at fifteen-years-old, so she's happy to see it. She so misses the fragrant smell of pine needles.

Samantha wants as many movies and pictures of Abigail as possible. Today, Abigail sleeps in the guest room where Joy stays. Rachel leads Samantha into the room not knowing that her Nana Cam is on. The room is dark as they enter.

"How are you Miss Abigail?" Samantha asks kneeling down to kiss her cheek.

"Who's that?" Rachel excitedly asks Abigail, moving closer.

Suddenly, the video camera's light comes on to startle Abigail. Samantha turns it off and tells them that funny, strange things always happen to her. Rachel winks and points to the angel light in the window before leaving. Strange things happen at their house too. Bear, their only surviving dog, follows her. His thick, fur coat is gone and Samantha thinks he looks odd.

Abigail begins to talk very quickly, as if to tell a secret before someone catches her.

"He got all shaved yesterday," says Abigail anxiously throwing little hands into the air, filled with concern.

"Do you like him that way?" Samantha asks.

Abigail replies, like an exasperated adult, while moving her little hands to and fro.

"He was leaving his hair all around the house. We pet him and his hair went all around the house. Every night we found them all the time with ..."

Her voice lowers making it impossible for Samantha to hear.

"Well, when you have things you love, you have to take care of them," Samantha announces with a hug.

Abigail continues in a whisper.

"Sassy passed away."

"Oh, I'm sorry. Sassy is with Daddy. That makes Daddy happy. Do you see Sassy with Daddy?"

Abigail gets quickly out of bed and grabs her new dolly, a gift from Grandma Joy. Bear barks in the living room so she runs out to see what's happening without answering.

James scoops her up as she tries to run past him. Samantha leaves the dark bedroom to greet Joy in the kitchen as James and Abigail move to the large, living room window. Joy looks years younger than she is.

"You're looking good," says Samantha as they hug.

Her video camera continues to tape the event. She's

the only one who knows it's on. Memorial posters Rachel made for Daniel's funeral grace walls and Samantha sees them for the first time. She's upset because there are no pictures of Daniel's side of the family. In fact, all the pictures of his family are gone from their usual place on the walls.

"Show Nana the new train set you got for Christmas," Joy tells Abigail.

Abigail has already started to open her pile of Christmas presents. Samantha pretends to turn on the already working Nana Cam to videotape the huge pile of gifts under the tree. Grandma Joy bought Abigail many of them, including a wide array of toy horses. Seeing them fills Samantha with dread. Samantha knows possessions will never replace the family Abigail seems to have lost. [43]

Abigail runs to the large, living room window as Joy walks outside to see horses ride past the house.

"Abigail saw a boy riding a big horse yesterday," Rachel notes.

"He had no shoes on his feet," says Abigail, placing hands on hips while visibly upset.

"Do you think he held on to the horse with his toes?" James asks jokingly from his spot on the couch.

An orb rises up from the seat beside James and drifts away. Rachel watches as Samantha looks at the walls.

"I changed the pictures to put new ones up," she announces as Samantha looks at long-forgotten photos with great surprise.

They are Daniel's infant pictures that Peter stole before the divorce.

"Peter gave them to Daniel when he lived with us," Rachel notes with a smile. "I made copies of that one to give to everybody," she says pointing as Samantha continues to stare at the wall.

Rebecca, Samuel, Terry, Ruth, and Grandma arrive. Samantha wonders how much longer she'll be able to video everyone without them knowing they're being filmed.

Samuel asks to play with the PlayStation game in her bedroom as Rachel hugs him. He played the game with Daniel for years. He quickly leaves the room disappointed and upset.

Samantha sets the video camera on a chair, in the breakfast nook, facing the Christmas tree. And then something odd happens. It looks like a dark gray mist comes from the top, right-hand corner, to cover the video camera display. The color stays somewhat as if the camera is switched to a still picture.

(Schwartz notes in *The Afterlife Experiments*, problems with recording equipment are common when one "connects with the realm of the spirit world." Video playback shows a screen with various hues of gray, and yellow, that lightens every so often for fourteen minutes. Family voices are clear but there are no visuals. Samantha later tests the camera, by putting the lens cap on while recording, but the video field remains black. She knows Daniel did not want her to video that segment of their time at Rachel's house.)

Samantha picks up the camera when she finally sees the gray screen and asks Abigail if she can video her. The video screen goes black before working normally.

"My camera has a mind of its own," says Samantha as she videotapes Bear lying on the cool floor.

He looks as if he's lost weight but it's hard to know for sure without his fur coat.

The video camera now focuses on the kitchen where James helps Rachel prepare food. Samantha has never seen him be so helpful. He spends more time in the kitchen helping today than in his entire life. Samantha doesn't know if it's because Daniel's spirit influences him or if he prefers to stay near Rachel. Ruth disrupts Samantha's train of thought, before it cascades ever downward, by calling her into the garage to see Rachel's new four-wheeler.

"My camera keeps doing strange things," Samantha whispers while walking towards Ruth. "It will be interesting to watch this video later."

Ruth impishly reveals a piece of Daniel's motorcycle now hidden in her pocket. For the first time, Samantha sees the red motorcycle her son rode before physical death. She can't imagine why Rachel keeps it. Grief overwhelms her.

Abigail enters the garage and quickly runs up to Samantha.

"I want to tell you something," she says. "Let's go outside."

Joy overhears her and stands between them as they move toward the screened-in back porch. She opens the sliding glass doors and they all move outside together. Joy sits calmly in a large camping chair, near the back door, as Abigail sits on a riding toy.

"What was it you wanted to tell me Abigail," Samantha asks.

Abigail looks down at the floor but doesn't answer.

"Why was it you wanted to come outside?"

Joy quickly replies.

"She likes to go outside."

Samantha knows that whatever Abigail wants to say will not be said in front of Joy. Rachel opens the sliding glass door and steps out.

"Oh, you're talking about these lights out here," she says pointing to the green and pink lights she and Abigail hung in the back yard.

A strip of multicolored light whizzes past the video camera lens as her sentence ends. It's a fast moving, unidentified object that makes a noise, somewhat like a model airplane, while flying past the top of the camera's range. Samantha knows it's Daniel's way of letting her know he's there.

"That's Daddy's chair," Abigail informs, pointing to one of two children's chairs.

The chairs are next to where Joy sits.

"Come here," says Abigail to Samantha.

"Can I take a picture?" Samantha asks.

She takes one of Abigail sitting on her toy a few feet away from Joy. Samantha looks at the digital picture and is surprised to see several orbs in it. The brightest orb is right above Joy's head.

"Do you want to see the picture," Samantha asks Abigail.

"Yes," Abigail replies adamantly.

"Look I did get a nice picture," Samantha says as Abigail looks at the camera display.

Abigail smiles with recognition so Samantha knows her granddaughter sees Daddy in his new form. (Samantha later counts more than twelve orbs all around Abigail as she looks at the picture again on her computer.)

"Take a picture of that," Abigail says pointing excitedly.

"You mean without you?"

"Yes."

Samantha snaps a picture of the two small chairs with Joy sitting next to them. Abigail starts walking towards Samantha.

"Oh, did you want to see it?"

"Yes," Abigail replies shaking her small head while looking at the camera display.

Samantha points to the tiny, bright orb above Daddy's little chair. She quietly asks, "Do you know what that is?"

Abigail smiles widely, shakes her little head yes, and walks away.

"You're a very smart girl," Samantha calls out.

Joy remains clueless that Abigail found a way to tell

her that she still sees Daddy.

James stands outside on the patio several feet away. Enthralled by a Cope's Gray Treefrog, he tries to get its picture. The frog sits still to stare at James. His first picture shows an orb to the right of the frog. The frog looks pure white because of the camera's flash. The third picture clearly shows the white spot, beneath the frog's eye, on the upper lip. The white spot is typical of this species of frog.

Suddenly, the doorbell rings as Rachel talks about Santa Claus. She arranged for a local Santa to give Abigail her first bike. Santa stays for less than ten minutes but delights everyone by the visit. Several pictures show orbs in them.

Abigail suddenly seems very shy when it's time to open the presents Daniel's family brought. Aunt Ruth quickly rips one open to show Abigail how the family opens presents. Samantha makes sure her first gift is the one she brought. Daniel gave her a small, stuffed, teddy bear last Mother's Day. The special mail order bear is dressed as if on vacation.

She wondered why he gave her such a gift but remembered the three-foot, furry bear Daniel gave her after a major operation in 1993. She felt his compassion then. James had gone fishing the day she got home from the hospital and she had been alone. Daniel made her promise not to give the bear to Samuel as he hugged her tightly.

"I might not be here all the time but you can hug the bear if you want to Momma," he said.

Samantha now hugged that big bear a lot. But she could not figure out why Daniel gave her the small one. She put it back inside its gift box, stored it in her closet, and promptly forgot about it. Daniel's spirit reminded her of the gift a week before their visit with Rachel and Abigail.

"It's for Abigail Mom," Samantha heard him say.

She understood perfectly and wrapped it up in Christmas paper. Daniel bought his daughter her Christmas present nearly a year before physical death.

As Abigail opens the gift, Samantha notes Daddy gave it to Nana. Now he wants Abigail to have it. Abigail is delighted.

"I named him Sunshine," she notes with a wink, "but you can pick a name for him."

Abigail removes the bear's sunglasses, puts them on her tiny, perfect nose, and says, "Cool Dude."

Daniel used the term frequently so Samantha knows she did the right thing. Her stunned family remains silent. They all remember Daniel, the "Cool Dude."

Samantha made everyone gifts of love. She felt driven the night before to give both Joy and Rachel small photo albums. During the night, she learned how to pull pictures of them, with friends and family, off of videos. Daniel wasn't in any of the pictures.

A small orb appears near Terry as Rachel opens presents from Samantha. It passes onto his face and disappears from view. Rachel begins to cry while flipping through her photo album. Samantha has no idea that she distanced herself from everyone. Friends she and Daniel knew are no longer part of her life. Tears roll down Rachel's face as Samantha tries to comfort her. She doesn't realize Daniel's spirit put the thought of making the albums in her mind. It's his way of telling Rachel to reconnect with friends and family.

Ruth takes the video camera as Samantha hugs Rachel tightly.

"Don't cry," she says quietly consoling her. "It's going to be okay."

"You're so good," Rachel replies still sobbing.

Samantha whispers in her ear.

"We're all good. It's just that some of us don't know it yet."

Samantha has no idea where the words come from and she's unsure of their meaning. Daniel's spirit, she'll realize later, channeled through her once again.

    Samuel plays games with Abigail on the back porch later. He's still angry about not being able to play with Uncle Daniel's game system but tries to hide it. He sits on a big, red ball in front of sliding glass doors, leading to Rachel's bedroom, where the PlayStation sits. Samantha takes a picture as he holds his hands up to play peek-a-boo.

    She transfers the day's pictures onto her computer upon returning home. It's amazing to recall how Daniel talked the family into buying her the perfect printer last year. Pictures and videotapes now verify his presence. A smoky, white mist appears in the picture of Samuel playing peek-a-boo with Abigail. A small spirit orb sits on his fingertip as he holds his hands over his face. The cloudy mist is in the bedroom beyond the closed, sliding glass door. There's no smoke in the house and no physical reason for the mist. Samantha thinks, Daniel's spirit was not happy that Samuel was unable to play with the game system he grew to love.

    Other photos show numerous spirit orbs. Samantha especially loves a picture of Rebecca holding Abigail while sitting in her bedroom. She took two pictures in succession then. The first shows Rebecca with eyes closed. The second reveals a bright, white orb directly in front of Rebecca's vision. Another smaller orb sits directly in front of Abigail's eyes.

    In yet another picture, Samuel holds an etch-a sketch in front of his face. On the screen he wrote, "not Samuel" with a smiley face below it. He's wearing a t-shirt that says "Bike Week" with the picture of a motorcycle.

    "Obviously," Samantha thinks, "he got the thought from Daniel's spirit."

*   41. At this time, Samantha feels separate from everyone else. Blaming others for how we feel happens when we think something is lacking in us. When we think we are not as "good" as others we tend to project our feelings unto them. Naomi is the perfect "mirror" or "shadow" for*

Samantha because they both demand perfection. Emmanuel's Book notes if we always insist on perfection it will stop our growth as souls. Accepting imperfection helps us to grow. Change begins within us, as we love the part of ourselves that we think is imperfect.

Our ego is happy to separate us from other people. It loves to see us accuse others of doing what we do, or feeling as we do. Thoughts of fear, guilt, shame, and humiliation are negative emotions in the ego's world but are unrecognized by God. The ego is pleased when people feel negative emotions such as guilt, shame, fear, and humiliation because it keeps us separate in human form.

Having negative emotions is a great way to ignore that this is a dream world. As noted in <u>A Course in Miracles</u>, "Projection is a confusion in motivation, and given this confusion, trust becomes impossible." There are no negative emotions in the Kingdom of God. The body's eyes are not the means to see the real world for they, as well as the rest of the body, are illusions. Everything they see "lends itself to thoughts of sin and guilt. While everything that God created is forever without sin and therefore is forever without guilt."

Treating people differently, based on different beliefs, takes us away from Oneness. Yet, there is no duality in God's Kingdom. There is One, simply One, and One is Love. God is Love and we are Love because we are a part of God.

There is no reason to put others down once we become aware of the Truth that God is within us. Although it seems very real to humans, in essence, we are not here. In essence, there is no we, no them, no us. There is only One in which we live, and move, and have all BEing.

Renard puts it simply. "There is only one ego appearing as many." The real world is what we see with our attitude. Unconscious guilt from thinking we are separate is healed <u>knowing</u> there is One. The act of asking God for help is vital to free oneself from the ego mind. It then becomes easier to stop projecting unconscious guilt as God shows the *way to One.*

In coming years, Samantha changes beliefs and ways of perceiving the world. She learns that individuals, who feel inferior to others like herself, do not realize we are all the same, part of the One. She will stop accusing others of wrongdoing to feed her own ego.

42. Having negative thoughts and acting out the separation ruse is really a call for help. All negative behavior is ultimately a call for love. When someone acts negatively, they offer you the opportunity to bless them.

A Course in Miracles notes, "Every attack is a call for His patience, since His patience can translate attack into blessing." "You need the blessing you can offer him. There is no way for you to have it except by giving it. This is the law of God, and it has no exceptions."

Samantha's ego uses the "poor me" and "intimidation" power plays to steal energy so it's easy to recognize when others do the same thing. She doesn't realize that we act badly because we're seeking love. We feel an unconscious separation from our true nature but cannot identify the need. It surfaces as a vague feeling that something is missing in life.

Once we're aware of our true nature, we get our energy from God and no longer feel the unconscious need to steal energy from others. God is within everyone but often, religious leaders explain God's will based on their beliefs. In *Celestine Prophecy*, James Redfield explains a bit about religions. Religion is meant to help nurture the relationship to One but many structured religions fall short of that goal. They may not show people how to find the God within everyone.

43. Samantha is again somewhat consoled to think Abigail's soul chose her life before birth. Emmanuel tells us souls choose the childhood environment that's most effective to bring into focus distortions our soul selected to work on in

this lifetime. The experiences we have "are there in the interest of truth and Light."

Possessions are nice to have but can become limitations. Unless someone does it for us, we have to take care of the things we own. We may value them more than their true worth, pulling us further away from our Creator. Having too many possessions is just one of the many other human diversions that limit our time spent connecting with God. The ego loves it when we pay more attention to possessions than to our True Source.

Things take our focus away from God on the human level. However, they end up instructing us and helping our consciousness to grow. Obstructions to God are painful, but once we realize this, we can move through them getting closer to God. Emmanuel notes, "In the faith of knowing that all things are moving towards God the obstructions take on a different meaning and form."

:-)

~ 21 ~
Christmas Holiday Ends

Things are tough to bear a week before Christmas. There's too much to do so Samantha decides to cut down on the workload once again. Daniel's spirit consoles as volunteer jobs end. James, still unemployed, fishes often as the roof continues to leak. Samantha remains in her room, behind the closed door.

The poverty of childhood still haunts her. She misses little things, did for nearly thirty years, to make Christmas special. Christmas guests arrived early, year after year, to enjoy the day wherever she lived. She made quiche for breakfast and other treats to quell their hunger while waiting for dinner. Always happy to welcome unexpected guests, even if strangers, she wrapped generic gifts and made Christmas stockings to keep them busy as she finished preparing dinner. Daniel and Rebecca played fun guessing games while opening small stocking gifts in later years.

Driven by what he refers to as mismanaged finances, James assumes checkbook duties for the first time in their seventeen-year marriage. Monthly charge card bills become the subject of much discussion making it difficult to shop. Whenever Samantha requests a check for doctor or dentist visits, James conveniently forgets.

Daniel's spirit keeps her busy with activity to avoid further thoughts of suicide. She decides to make family photo albums for Christmas. The dollar store holds everything needed but cash seems impossible to get. A small rebate check in the mail soon answers repeated prayers.

Jude visits on Christmas Eve with his daughter, a month younger than Abigail is. Daniel and Rachel took Jude in when he decided to break free from the rigors of crack cocaine. Daniel got Jude a job and they lived and worked together for several years. Having used cocaine himself, and having other friends and an uncle addicted to crack, Daniel knew how hard it was to stop the habit. Addiction remained a huge issue, for many loved ones depended on drugs, or alcohol, to forget about their life.

Today is Jude's tenth anniversary of being "clean" and he happily reports that Daniel congratulated him while smiling in a dream. Samantha quickly tells him it wasn't "just a dream." Daniel's soul broke though the veil to communicate. Jude listens intently as she recalls the dream shared with Rebecca in New York. She announces that Daniel's soul was ready to leave its physical host. He spent most of his life trying to help people, and now, there's no need to mourn over the loss of him, for he lives on in another form. Jude, she quickly notes, gave Daniel another chance to help himself by helping someone else.

Samantha's head spins upon thinking of family and friends who continue to fight drug or alcohol addiction. Daniel's attempts to help Uncle Amos break addiction remain unsuccessful. Samantha now senses his soul communicating with Amos who still sits in jail. (44)

Samantha decides to make the usual sage, turkey stuffing and bake quiche because her family requests it. For the first time, James helps her in the kitchen by chopping onions and celery. He makes a Key lime pie for dessert as well. Samantha smiles to think that Daniel's soul still affects him.

Rebecca and Samuel arrive early Christmas morning. After voicing surprise over the missing Christmas tree, they open presents quietly. The foursome watch television for hours before going to Ruth and Naomi's for dinner.

Samantha's pictures remain ignored for no one voices interest over unexplainable phenomena. Today she decides to try again by showing Rebecca pictures of last weeks visit with Rachel and Abigail.

"I wonder if she dumped the PlayStation game, got

rid of it," Samantha says handing the camera to James to pass to Rebecca.

Rebecca recognizes Daniel's essence upon seeing Samuel, sitting on the red ball with the smoky mist beyond Rachel's bedroom doors.

"Wow," Rebecca says upon seeing the picture, "spirit energy."

She hands the camera back to silent James, who thinks both women are crazy.

Christmas dinner disappoints Samantha. She misses surprise and welcome guests and seeing the delight of people upon opening Christmas stocking gifts. Family members pass most of their eight hours of time outside around the patio table. A lone motorcycle rider periodically drives past the house. And every time it does, Samantha yearns for Daniel. Everyone happily takes their quiche when it's time to return home but Samantha still feels empty.

Daniel's presence permeates the atmosphere later as she reviews the Christmas video and pictures. Spirit orbs sit in many photos and white lights are brighter in some. A beautiful fuscia colored orb appears on her video as the family laughs together. Samantha knows Daniel's spirit was again moving, from house to house, to visit loved ones.

The 2004 Indian Ocean earthquake occurs the next day as Abigail turns three-years-old (http://en.wikipedia.org/wiki/2004_Indian_Ocean_earthquake). The earthquake triggers devastating tsunamis killing more than 225,000 people in eleven countries. It's one of the deadliest natural disasters in history, at the time, and the second largest earthquake ever recorded. It causes the earth to vibrate, triggers other earthquakes, and is estimated to have released the energy of 23,000 Hiroshima-type atomic bombs (http://news.nationalgeographic.com/news/2004/12/1227_041226_tsunami.html).

Samantha remains grateful to communicate with Daniel even if she can't change the things he warns about.

Having the information ahead of disasters helps her to prepare mentally and verifies her connection to the Otherside. She still warns family of increasing bouts of severe weather conditions even though they don't believe her. They're only interested in local storms.

The family's disbelief in greater realities continues. No one seems to believe in Daniel's spirit. Now Samantha jokes upon sensing Daniel's presence, especially if Rebecca is near.

"What's that Timmy?" She often remarks with a nod of her head. "Lassie fell in the well?"

Rebecca is not pleased that her mother thinks it funny.

Her lovely daughter hosts the family's New Year's Eve so Samantha quickly decides to bring copies of pictures. The printer Daniel talked the family into giving her does all the things needed to process them. It holds slots for camera disks, making it easy to print them, put them into her computer, or make copies. She uses the printer to scan pictures into her computer as well.

This New Year's Eve, the small gathering consists of Rebecca, Samuel, Ruth, Naomi, Terry, James, and Samantha. As usual, James moves inside with Samuel to watch television. The rest of the family begins to play pinochle as "Take it to the Limit" starts to play. As she starts to sing, the CD player begins to act erratically. Samantha announces Daniel's presence. Rebecca rises to change the CD.

"It only messes up when you're by the CD player," Terry notes gruffly, with an angry glare at Samantha when it happens again.

She tells them Daniel has lots of stops to make.

Even knowing Daniel's alcohol level was way beyond the legal limit to drive when he had his accident, no one stops drinking.

"Daniel told me to do this," Rebecca says while pouring everyone a shot of Jack Daniels.

Samantha swears to never drink it again after they toast with the vile tasting whiskey. Already on her third rum and coke, she looks at Rebecca as they continue to play cards.

"I'm not going back," she says with a smirk.

Rebecca is the only one who understands as silence fills the room. Samantha plans to stay open to unseen forces. But there's a lot to learn. She remains unaware that words, and actions, make a difference in what she experiences.

Samantha, Rebecca jokingly now reminds the family, got a scratch off lotto ticket for Christmas. She didn't check the fake lotto ticket, making the bearer think they'd won, but spoiled the joke.

"I'm not meant to be rich in this life," she said handing it to James. "I'm meant to pave the way for you all."

Samuel goes to his room. James moves slowly back to his station, alone on the couch. After staying up the night before, until midnight, and waking to fish at 4:00 AM, he is exhausted. He dozes in front of the television after helping Rebecca open her second bottle of wine. The rest of the family continues to play cards on the porch. Samantha's Nana Cam videos a small orb as they continue to drink and make fun of Samantha. They mock her by saying Daniel's responsible for everything that happens around them.

Fed-up, she shows pictures of spirit orbs taken during their visit to see Rachel and Abigail. Silence again shrouds the room like a thick fog. Now as Samantha takes pictures, she shows them to Rebecca pointing out orbs. One photo shows a greenish mist with visible orbs in and around it.

"Mom you're camera was one of the first digital camera's to come out and it's old now," Rebecca notes with disgust. "There's nothing mystical about it. It's a piece of shit now."

Terry tries to take Samantha's picture as she talks but the camera refuses to work.

"Some pictures," she says smiling graciously, "are

not meant to be taken until the right moment."
She assumes that moment is when Daniel's spirit sits in position.
"I'm writing a book now for Abigail about her daddy," Samantha says with authority after a swig of her drink.
She has lost her mind. The family is certain.
A nearby bridge begins to raise as the Jungle Queen sounds its horn. It's before midnight and the boat holds many guests. Always fond of "mooning," Terry runs to the water's edge. Samantha videotapes as Terry pulls down his pants to moon the crowd.
"Happy New Year, Happy New Year," he yells, wagging his white butt back and forth.
The boat's guests roar with laughter, hoots, and applause.
Another shot of alcohol swims down their throats as James drifts, in and out of sleep, on the couch. Samuel, who remains inside, decides to lock them out of the house shortly before midnight. *"Nothing Else Matters"* plays in the background.
Samantha sings but she has no idea what the words will mean in future years.
"So close, no matter how far, couldn't be much more from the heart. Forever trust in who we are and nothing else matters."
Samantha and Rebecca soon yell at Samuel to open the sliding glass door. They both have an urgent need to use the bathroom. Samuel refuses from the kitchen and leaves the room as James moves in. Falling down drunken Terry threatens to break through the small kitchen window.
"You better open the door or I'll pop the f**king window," he snarls jerking towards the glass. "You don't think so? I've done it before cause I got my ass stuck between these windows. You want to see?"
He laughs heartily while grabbing the window frame

to steady him.

Terry begins to open the window frame wider as the family roars with laughter. James quickly opens the sliding glass door and starts back to the couch.

"Is that your fun for the evening?" Samantha asks.

A fuscia colored orb drifts from the wall, passes over James' head, and moves into the living room.

It' now 11:45 PM. They decide to call Rachel to avoid the midnight rush. Rachel sounds genuinely happy to hear from them. She invites them to Abigail's' belated birthday party, where she might get her first horse. Rachel believes the miniature horse is perfect for Abigail.

Midnight fireworks begin as the family toasts with cheap champagne. Samuel and James shoot fireworks in the yard for several minutes. Although they all miss Daniel, most of them are so drunk they don't think about him. By 12:30 AM, James and Samuel are back in the living room. Other family members try to play cards.

Samantha takes pictures of Samuel and James during trips to the bathroom. A shot of James sleeping on the couch becomes one of her favorite photos. The large, white, spirit orb, directly above his head, is hard to miss. The orb is the essence of either Daniel or James's dad, Zephaniah, who died in the house years ago. Either way, she knows spirits from the Otherside are there for the New Year.

The card game ends before two o'clock in the morning. A sober Naomi drives Ruth and Terry home. James returns home alone as Samantha stays to be with Rebecca and Samuel. Her health has worsened and she knows their marriage is over. The negativity at her house is just too stressful and it's only a matter of time before they divorce. Daniel's spirit continues to warn of worldwide changing weather patterns. But she knows his essence will continue to guide her safely into exciting, unknown territory. She looks forward to knowing more about the Otherside.

Samantha believes physical death lies just beyond the horizon for health continues to limit everyday activities. Next year, she'll read *Emmanuel's Book*. As noted in the text, "Your body in illness is not your enemy but your faithful friend. It has been programmed by your soul to react in that exact way at that exact time."

Her soul will stretch immensely during the next several years as she reestablishes a connection to the God within. She'll embrace the gifts of Clairsentience, Clairaudience, Clairvoyance and Inspirational Thought. These gifts are within every human being on earth. Two years later, she will read:

"This is a schoolroom of illusion. Do not give permanent reality to temporary things. Once you have learned what you came to learn the illusion can be left."

Samantha will eventually leave the illusion behind as she begins a new life of teaching.

44. Everything on earth has a purpose. Emmanuel notes, "The family is a hothouse for spiritual growth." Illnesses such as substance addictions are one of many choices the soul makes before birth. Sometimes we choose these illnesses to help other souls with their growth. Learning lessons such as compassion helps our soul's evolution.

:-)

Epilogue

We seem to live within a dream. If your dream is unwanted or appears as a nightmare, you have the power to change it. How you look at things makes a huge difference. This difference affects other people, other lives, and dimensions we can only imagine.

There is only Now. Each day lived in the Now is another opportunity to help all spirits get back Home. Like humans, every day is unique and filled with possibility. This unique nature makes it even more vital to live each day in the Now, for it only happens once.

A common question is, when you look at a glass that is fifty percent full, how do you perceive it? Samantha always saw the glass as half empty. She trained her brain to see a half full glass, which continues to fill with each change in awareness of Reality. We will be Home when we all picture the glass as brimming over, filling other glasses, and merging into the Oneness of which we truly are.

Samantha's changing attitude helps her to rise beyond the external factors of life. Future books continue to document her saga as spiritual awareness increases, by looking at each drama with a new perspective. As noted by Alan Cohen, M.A. (alancohen.com), energy and happiness have a lot to do with what is going on inside you. Although environment and physical factors may influence us, attitude makes or breaks us. The power to rise beyond the dream is yours. Use it wisely.

:-)

Bibliography

* Baldwin S. *Dying to Live Again-Channeled Interviews With Souls From The Otherside*. 2001.

* Brungardt-Pope H. *For the Aspiring Mystic*. 2001.

* Chadwick G. *Reincarnation and Your Past-Life Memories*. 1998.

* Carter J. *Nasty People ...How to Stop Being Hurt By Them Without Becoming One of Them*. 1989.

* Dyer W. *Pulling Your Own Strings*. 1978.

* Edwards J. *One Last Time*. 1999.

* Emerson RW. *Emerson's Essays*. 1926, 1951.

* Emoto M. *The Hidden Messages in Water*. 2004.

* Foundation for Inner Peace. *A Course in Miracles*. 1976, 1992.

* Guggenheim B, Guggenheim H. *Hello from Heaven: A New Field of Research-After-Death Communication Confirms That Life and Love Are Eternal*. 1997.

* Hay L. *The Power is Within You*. 1991.

* Holmes E. *The Science of Mind. Original Text* 1926, 1998.

* "   " *The Science of Mind*. 1938, 1998.

* "   " *This Thing Called You*. 1948.

* Kubler-Ross E. *On Death and Dying*. 1969.

* Law Nolte's D. *Children Learn What They Live*. 1954.

* McCarthy JS. *The Connection Between Energy Lines, the Orb Phenomenon, Dimensions and UFOs'*. 2007.

* Millman D. *The Life You Were Born to Live*. 1995.

* Monroe RA. *Journeys Out of the Body.* 1971, 1977.
* " " *Far Journeys.* 1992.
* " " *Ultimate Journey.* 1996.
* Morse M. *Transformed by the Light.* 1993.
* Newton M. *Destiny of Souls.* 2000.
* Page C. *Spiritual Alchemy.* 2003.
* Rodegast P, Stanton J. *Emmanuel's Book.* 1985.
* Redfield J. *Celestine Prophecy.* 1993.
* " " *The Secret of Shambhala.* 1999.
* Renard GR. *The Disappearance of The Universe.* 2002.
* Rinpoche S. *"The Tibetan Book of Living and Dying."* Audio Literature: 1993.
* Schwartz G. *The Afterlife Experiments.* 2002.
* Spalding BT. *Life and Teaching of the Masters of the Far East: Volume V.* 1955.
* Todeschi KJ. *"Kevin Todeschi at Wild Acres".* Southern Lights Newsletter, Spring 2008: page 6. (seare.org)
* " " *Edgar Cayce on Soul Mates: Unlocking the Dynamics of Soul Attraction.* 1999.
* Troward T. *The Edinburgh & Dore Lectures on Mental Science.* 1904; 1909.
* Van Praagh J. *Talking to Heaven.* 1999.
* Weiss B. *Many Lives, Many Masters.* 1988.
* " " *Through Time Into Healing.* 1993.

About the Author

SAM's compelling journey of rising from the projects, of Detroit, to living on her own at fifteen led to the realization that there must be more to life. A near-death experience at age sixteen helped to spur interest in the unseen world. Since that time, SAM has aggressively searched for answers to questions asked throughout the ages. The awareness that we are spirits, in human form having a physical experience, came after her son's transition on April 4, 2004.

Involved in the nutritional aspects of hiv/aids care from 1988 to 2008, she is a strong advocate of human rights and nutritional services. SAM served the public and private sector by volunteering in a variety of Federal, State and County positions. She authored and co-authored numerous articles on nutrition and hiv/aids, was the Nutrition Editor for NUMEDX HIV and NUMEDX Hepatitis, and co-authored *HIV Medications Food Interactions (And So Much More)*.

SAM, author of the "Lightworker's Log Book Series," is an ordained minister, channel of higher realms, teacher, founder of SAM I AM PROductions (samiamproductions.com), and administrator of the popular Internet resource, Lightworker's Log (LightworkersLog.com). Spreading Spirit's message of Oneness throughout the globe, SAM is a wayshower helping others to learn the truth of BEing so humanity can return unique figments back to *All That Is*.

The Lightworker's Log Book Series

Death of the Sun

A Change in Perception

Lightworker's Log: Transformation

Manifesting

Prayer Treatments

Adventures in Greece and Turkey

Earth Angels

Return to Light :-) John of God Helps

Bits of Wisdom

Book of One :-) Volume 1

Book of One :-) Volume 2

Book of One :-) Volume 3

www.ingramcontent.com/pod-product-compliance
Lightning Source LLC
Chambersburg PA
CBHW020927090426
42736CB00010B/1067